Pra for

"More than 20 yea   ago ʜod gave me the privilege of friendship with the Boose family in a little military chapel in North Carolina. Watching Cindy raise their girls and walk with the Lord I saw her curiosity and deliberateness. Curiosity about life and faith that drove her to scripture, and deliberateness in her application of it with their young family. Since then, her curiosity has become wisdom, and her deliberateness has produced a generation of wise young women.

In this devotional she doesn't only share her insights from Hebrews but invites to deeper engagement over effective faith. I hope that you will "sweat" a little with me through the timely challenges of 52 Days of Faith."

— *Vern Salter*
Counseling and Soul Care, The Navigators

"Once again Cindy Boose nails it. 52 Days of Faith goes deep for the spiritually mature yet is understandable and usable for those new in the faith. Each day has a solid scripture reference that Cindy explains in an engaging manner. She then tops it off with questions to ponder, bringing God's word as an applicable and important part of our daily lives. Read this book! You won't be disappointed."

— *Kip McCormick*
Pastor, Author, Colonel US Army retired

Praise for 52 Days of Faith

Cindy Boose has written a lovely devotional book entitled *52 Days of Faith*. She has provided daily thoughts based on scripture passages that deal with critical questions in life. She fills her homilies with stories from gardening and home ownership to life in the workplace. She uses these simple stories from real everyday life to illustrate the key truths of scripture, dealing with death, the Lordship of Christ, giving glory to God in all circumstances, and many more.

I take one example, her homily on the shared humanity of Jesus. Many years ago, I heard a former Muslim say that he, "could not worship a God who did not understand human suffering." This is what brought him to Christ. Cindy Boose paints a wonderful portrait of a Savior who took on all our sorrows and as God in the flesh has experienced all our sufferings and far more. Her meditation on Hebrews 2:14-18 is a moving example of her writing skill and desire to draw people closer in their devotion to Jesus.

I highly recommend this little volume as a new opportunity for Christians everywhere to deepen their daily walk with Christ.

—*Dr. David Cashin*
Columbia International University

52 Days of Faith

Also by Cindy Boose

52 Days of Grace

52 Days of Faith
A devotional based on Paul's letter to the Hebrews

Cindy Boose

52 Days of Faith
Copyright © 2019 Cindy Boose

Photography and makeup by Anna Boose

Cover design by Paul Strand

ISBN: 9781797578132

Printed in the United States of America

Independently published
http://cindyspostscripts.blogspot.com

To my dear mother who now enjoys the end result of her faith in the presence of her Lord and Savior Jesus Christ. I love you, Mom.

Table of Contents

Acknowledgments

I must start by giving honor and glory to the Lord for His perfect timing and wonderful plan of which I know nothing. If it wasn't for Him, I would have plowed ahead and published this book before the proper time, missing out on all the pruning and subsequent growth He had in store for me as His child.

I also must take note of my dear husband, Donald, whose support and timely words of wisdom have encouraged me more than he could ever know: I love you. And to my four daughters who always seem to know the right thing to say and the right time to say it; thank you for your help and support, lovely ladies, as well as to my kind and loving son-in-law, Luke.

To my mother who suddenly reached the end of her time here on earth, I miss you more than I ever thought possible. Dad, you bring much joy and laughter to my life, I appreciate your guidance and common-sense advice over the years, even though you always thought I never listened. Without you two, I would not be the woman I am today. I love you both!

To my sister Susan whom I've had the pleasure of getting to know so much better during the past few years, you always challenge me to slow down and enjoy the ride, and to my little sister, Debby, I've always looked up to you as an older sister and you inspire me to love deeply and serve freely.

My heartfelt gratitude goes to my gracious friend Diane, a passionate follower of Jesus Christ, who is always ready to help me in whatever way necessary, and to all those readers in the Body of Christ over the years whose encouraging words and godly feedback drive me to my knees in praise to our great God.

To my brothers and sisters of the Cordata Court Bible study, your eagerness to see the next book published motivated me to push through the finish line. Your hunger for God's Word, willingness to accept your lot in life, and love for the Lord inspires me.

Once again, I must give a hearty thanks to Paul Strand for his painstaking attention to detail to bring this book to life. I appreciate your hard work.

Finally, I end where I have started with expressing my gratitude to Jesus Christ my Lord and Savior who grows absolutely more precious to me as the years go by. Thank you for the gift of Yourself. I love you, Jesus.

1
Relentless Pursuit

"In the past God spoke to our ancestors through the prophets at many times and in various ways, but in these last days he has spoken to us by his Son, whom he appointed heir of all things, and through whom also he made the universe" (Hebrews 1:1-2).

God is always pursuing us. His greatest desire is to be involved in our lives and to share in our struggles. As a result, He has always made a way to communicate with His image bearers. Once He sent prophets, brave men and women who would speak His Word to a wayward people, deliver hard truths meant to draw His own back to Him, and provide a means of corresponding with those He loves while reaching out to those who don't even know Him.

Now that we have the benefit of Jesus who willingly set aside His divine identity to become flesh for a time, fully God and fully man, we have a new way to converse with God. Through faith in the Son of God we have the very Spirit of God dwelling within us. No longer do we need to go through a messenger. We have direct access to our Father-- what a glorious gift.

This means He will deliver His Word directly to us when we are straying, expressing hard truths to our hearts to draw us back to Him, and constantly pursue us in a special, intimate way that is hard to ignore. Furthermore, this Spirit does more than just communicate. As Oswald Chambers explains, ". . . when I am born again by the Spirit of God, I know that Jesus Christ did not come only to *teach*--He came to *make me what He teaches I should be . . .*"

> *God relentlessly pursues us so we can live*
> *the abundant life He created us to live through*
> *the power of the indwelling Spirit of God*
> *delivered by faith in Jesus Christ.*

What difference does God's indwelling Spirit make in your everyday life?

_____

_____

What kind of amazing love does your Father have for you that He would give you such intimate access to Him?

_____

_____

When is it easy for you to ignore His relentless pursuit of your heart?

_____

_____

Heavenly Father,

I am so thankful for Your amazing love that drives You to pursue me, an unholy, sinful creature. What an unspeakable gift you have given me in Your Spirit living within. I confess, I don't always pay attention to Your promptings nor tap into Your power over sin and I rarely cooperate with You as You attempt to transform me. Help me to surrender all to You so that I can experience more fully the benefits of Your loving pursuit of me.
In Jesus' Name I pray, Amen.

52 Days of Faith

2
Conduit

"In the past God spoke to our ancestors through the prophets at many times and in various ways, but in these last days he has spoken to us by his Son, whom he appointed heir of all things, and through whom also he made the universe" (Hebrews 1:1-2).

The rays of light dazzle my eyes as they hit the drops of water forming on the velvety rose petals. Birds flit through the bushes, making a pleasant background melody for my daily chore. The rich, tilled soil eagerly accepts the flow of life-giving liquid coming from the hose as the scent of the fertile loam rises to tickle my nose. Watering the garden is one of my favorite things to do.

Without a hose, delivering water to my plants would be nearly impossible. I could use a bucket or a watering can, but the job is done with much more efficiency and accuracy by using a channel through which to deliver the water.

Likewise, we are unable to receive any of the good things God has for us on our own. As sinners fallen from our intended place in the presence of a God who loves us, our transgressions have created a chasm that exists between God and mankind, blocking the flow of blessings and goodness He desires to give us. We need some kind of delivery system that can bridge that uncrossable gap.

Jesus is this conduit through whom we experience all things: Creation, intimacy with a holy God, righteousness by faith, salvation from eternal death as well as deliverance of an abundant life. Without Jesus, nothing would exist. Apart from Christ, we have no hope of connecting to the God who cherishes us but is unable to abide with our ever-present sin. Exclusive of God's Son, we cannot get right with God nor avoid the punishment our sins deserve. On our own, our lives are empty and meaningless.

Fifteenth century priest, monk and writer, Thomas A. Kemp, succinctly captured the importance of Jesus as the way, the truth, and the life. "Without the way there is no going; without the truth there is no knowing; without the life there is no living."

Jesus is our only hope and our greatest treasure.

How do you get off track, thinking you can get to God through your own righteousness, effort or good intentions?

When do you minimize the work Christ did for you on the cross?

_____

_____

How can you honor Jesus by the way you live your life?

_____

_____

Heavenly Father,

You made a way for me to get to You in sending Your Son to an ungrateful world in order to die a criminal's death. Without Jesus nothing would even exist, yet I often deny His importance in my desire to live apart from Your grace. Help me to remember my dire dependence upon Jesus for my life, my righteousness, my salvation; my all. Give me the strength to surrender all to Jesus.

In Jesus' name I pray, Amen

3

God Revealed

"The Son is the radiance of God's glory and the exact representation of his being, sustaining all things by his powerful word. After he had provided purification for sins, he sat down at the right hand of the Majesty in heaven" (Hebrews 1:3).

No one has ever seen God or His glory and lived to tell about it (Exodus 33:20; John 1:18). His ways are as mysterious to us as the sinking of Atlantis or the whereabouts of Amelia Earhart (Isaiah 55:8-9). Due to the holy nature of God, I have no hope of entering into a relationship with Him because of my sin (Isaiah 59:2-3).

As difficult as it is to get to know God, Jesus has made it possible to do just that. When Jesus set aside His divinity to take on the form of a man, He introduced the world to the magnificence of God's glory, giving us the opportunity to see for ourselves the splendor and beauty of His Light (John 1:14). Jesus also gave us the ability to discover the nature of this all-powerful God. He Himself is His exact imprint, the very image of God's character.

But Jesus is not just a clone of some kind or an idol who is simply fashioned after God. He is God Himself and holds all things together by the power of His word. Since we have been given such a glorious gift as Jesus – meaning God with us -- let's not waste one single moment. Let us take every opening we've been granted to find out more about our Lord and grow closer to Him. May we invite Him into every part of our lives, giving Him access to even the most intimate and shameful parts. It is then that we will truly appreciate the sacrifice Jesus made for us, taking advantage of the chance we've been given to live in relationship with a holy God.

Twentieth-century Christian writer and teacher, Watchman Nee, knew the importance of Christ to our lives, both physically and spiritually. He said, "God will answer all our questions in one way and one way only—namely, by showing us more of His Son."

If we want to know God, we need look no further than Jesus.

Do you ever feel isolated, unable to catch a glimpse of the God who loves you?

_____

_____

When do you try to reach God in your own goodness or by your own effort, forsaking the sacrifice Jesus made to provide such access to God?

_____

_____

How are you wasting the precious gift of a relationship with God through faith in Jesus Christ by spending time in worldly or fleshly pursuits in an effort to find the fulfillment that only comes from knowing God?

_____

_____

Heavenly Father,

I admit of my need for Jesus but also of my tendency to squander the gift I've been given. I often fail to take advantage of the opening to know You more intimately that You have given me through Christ. Help me to see the value in knowing You more and give me boldness in making You known to those who are lost. Thank You for the precious gift of Jesus Christ my Lord.
I pray these things in Jesus' Name, Amen.

4

Impotent Jesus

"For to which of the angels did God ever say, 'You are my Son; today I have become your Father?'

Or again, 'I will be his Father, and he will be my Son?' And again, when God brings his firstborn into the world, he says, 'Let all God's angels worship him.'

In speaking of the angels he says, 'He makes his angels spirits, and his servants flames of fire.'

But about the Son he says, 'Your throne, O God, will last for ever and ever; a scepter of justice will be the scepter of your kingdom. You have loved righteousness and hated wickedness; therefore God, your God, has set you above your company-ions by anointing you with the oil of joy.'

He also says, 'In the beginning, Lord, you laid the foundations of the earth, and the heavens are the work of your hands. They will perish, but you remain; they will all wear out like a garment. You will roll them up like a robe; like a garment they will be changed. But you remain the same, and your years will never end.'

To which of the angels did God ever say, 'Sit at my right hand until I make your enemies a footstool for your feet?'

Are not all angels ministering spirits sent to serve those who will inherit salvation?" (Hebrews 1:5-14).

"We are pulling our children out of your afterschool program because our family doesn't believe in Jesus." As much as these words hurt, knowing that the three precious boys who had accepted the gospel of Christ would no longer attend Bible study in our home, I had to respect this father's decision. At least the man understood who we were proclaiming Jesus to be and had taken his position. Most in today's culture does not take such a stand but would rather portray Jesus as an impotent man or some kind of lunatic. Neither assessment lines up with the truth of scripture. In the end, we will all be held accountable for what we did with the reality of Jesus Christ.

Many things have been said about Jesus: He was a good man, or teacher of morality, or prophet. His true identity, however, is often played-down or denied.

God leaves no room for doubt in the distinct character of Jesus Christ. He clearly defines His sonship, divinity, supremacy, power, majesty, honor and eternal nature. Jesus has authority to judge, heal, forgive sins, proclaim good news, grant freedom, bind up the brokenhearted, release those held captive, comfort, exchange ashes for beauty and mourning for joy. As Creator, Jesus has power over sickness and the laws of nature; making Him able to heal the ill, calm the storm, give sight to the blind, mobility to the lame, stop a freight train, or change the trajectory of a bullet.

With such a Jesus before me, I have a decision to make. Will He be my teacher who gives me sound advice and sets a good example for me to follow, or will He be my Lord and Savior, the only one able to free me from the punishment of my sin that has doomed me to eternal death? One makes Him impotent, the other exalts His name above all others. One reduces His sacrifice to a fairy tale, the other honors Him in His place at the right hand of God. One makes Him a mere man sent by God, the other makes Him God.

Here, God leaves no room for speculation. Popular culture and fringe religious sects claim Jesus as savior yet rob Him of His divinity. They may claim to respect Jesus, but there is more to Him than sheer humanity. How I view Jesus, and then what I do with Him, tells the tale of my assessment of Him. If He is only a man to me, how can He possibly save me, or heal me, or help me, or give me abundant life? Only a divine, eternal Jesus has the power to do such things.

All to Jesus I surrender,
all to Him I freely give;
I would ever love and trust Him,
in His presence daily live.
I surrender all, I surrender all;
All to Thee my Blessed Savior,
I surrender all.
— J. Van De Venter

What do you really believe about Jesus? Have you taken a stand for Him or against Him?

_____

_____

When do your actions betray the true state of your faulty assessment of Jesus when He is really Healer, Comforter and Deliverer from the power of sin?

_____

_____

How are you failing to trust Jesus as your Divine Savior?

_____

_____

Heavenly Father,

I admit I often minimize the identity of Jesus in my assessment of His character. I frequently place Him in a category as wise philosopher, mystic guru, or kind and humble man instead of acknowledging His divine, eternal and all-powerful nature. Give me a true assessment of Jesus and help me agree with what You have revealed about His character through Scripture. May I willingly bow at His feet as my Lord and Savior.
In Jesus' Name I pray, Amen.

5

The Threat of Death

"Since the children have flesh and blood, he too shared in their humanity so that by his death he might break the power of him who holds the power of death—that is, the devil—and free those who all their lives were held in slavery by their fear of death" (Hebrews 2:14-15).

Everyone faces it but no one wants to talk about it. It's our shared experience as humans but we all pretend it isn't there. We live as if it won't happen but constantly work to prevent its coming. As Ben Franklin's saying goes, "Nothing is certain except death and taxes."

Death: it looms over our consciousness, reminding us of its presence whenever a health crisis occurs, or we experience a close call on the road, or a loved one dies. It's inevitable, but mysterious and scary. As writer David Gerrold said, "Life is hard. Then you die. Then they throw dirt in your face. Then the worms eat you. Be grateful it happens in that order." We can all laugh at his fatalistic attitude, but it reveals what's at the core of our fears: Death is coming. It's bad and there's nothing we can do about it.

While we may be powerless against the inevitability of death, Jesus chose to face death in order to liberate us from its certainty. He willingly placed Himself in the hands of death so that we would not have to taste its bitter tang. He entered into the realm of death and in the words of Welsh preacher Peter Joshua, "When death stung Jesus Christ, it stung itself to death."

Through faith in Jesus Christ, then, we can be free from the worry of what will happen when this life is over. Instead of facing the inevitable, we can look forward to what Jesus is preparing for us beyond. He faced death so we wouldn't have to.

No longer is death a certainty,
In Christ, life goes on for an eternity

In what ways do you live with the constant fear of death coloring your every waking moment?

_____

_____

Do you trust in Jesus so that you can live without the fear of death?

_____

_____

When are you afraid to live because you don't want to die?

_____

_____

Heavenly Father,

You sent Jesus to die the death meant for me. As a result, I can live without the fear of death. Still, I often let its ugly stench taint my life, keeping me from living as You meant me to live. Help me to trust you enough to know that Jesus has removed the threat of death, freeing me from that familiar fear. Give me the strength to choose to live the abundant life for which Jesus died, so that I could live. Give me eyes to see the goodness You have prepared for me at the end of this temporal life.
In Jesus' Name I pray, Amen

6
Shared Humanity

"Since the children have flesh and blood, he too shared in their humanity so that by his death he might break the power of him who holds the power of death — that is, the devil — and free those who all their lives were held in slavery by their fear of death. For surely it is not angels he helps, but Abraham's descendants. For this reason he had to be made like them, fully human in every way, in order that he might become a merciful and faithful high priest in service to God, and that he might make atonement for the sins of the people. Because he himself suffered when he was tempted, he is able to help those who are being tempted" (Hebrews 2:14-18).

When going through hard times we all want to talk to someone who can relate to our misery: Someone who has experienced what we are currently suffering, who has felt the full weight of our burdens, someone who can understand.

A study released in the July 2014 issue of the *Journal of Personality and Social Psychology* found that those going through hard times or experiencing anxiety and depression prefer their feelings to be validated rather than to hear positive messages of encouragement and optimism. We prefer empathy over a pep talk, a compassionate listening ear more than an upbeat word of optimism, and understanding better than hearing truth. As the saying goes, "Misery loves company." Most of us don't want to be fixed, but just want to be understood.

Roman philosopher Lucius Annaeus Seneca said, "One of the most beautiful qualities of true friendship is to understand and to be understood." Jesus, who became fully human and as a result experienced suffering and temptation on a level we cannot begin to fathom, is uniquely qualified to understand our current difficulties. No one else is better able to come to our aid, providing comfort we would otherwise never experience.

Because of what Jesus went through while here on earth, He can provide sympathy when we most need it, helping to relieve our suffering and giving us the strength to stand firm when we feel like giving in. Jesus is our compassionate and faithful High Priest.

No matter our circumstances we can trust Jesus because He understands.

How do you avoid Jesus when temptation weighs heavily upon you, thinking He couldn't possibly understand what you're going through?

_____

_____

When are you most apt to "go it alone" instead of turning to Jesus for help?

_____

_____

What is your greatest temptation and how do you tend to conceal it instead of exposing it to Jesus?

_____

_____

Heavenly Father,

I admit I often think I am in this all alone and that no one could possibly understand what I'm going through. Thank you for sending your Son, who being tempted in every way can uniquely empathize with my struggles, giving me the opportunity to receive true support and understanding. Help me to always keep the lines of communication open with Him, so that I never have to go it alone. Thank you for your loving mercy displayed in the form of Jesus Christ.
In Jesus' name I pray, Amen

52 Days of Faith

7

The Pedestal

"Therefore, holy brothers and sisters, who share in the heavenly calling, fix your thoughts on Jesus, whom we acknowledge as our apostle and high priest. He was faithful to the one who appointed him, just as Moses was faithful in all God's house. Jesus has been found worthy of greater honor than Moses, just as the builder of a house has greater honor than the house itself" (Hebrews 3:1-3).

When I lived in South Carolina with my family, our home was a quick one-hour drive from Charlotte, NC where the Billy Graham Library was located. Going through this exhibit, seeing Billy's childhood home, and hearing stories about his faithfulness to God gave me even more respect for the man whose crusade ministry was responsible for my own salvation. Because of his faithfully-lived life, it would be easy for me to place Billy Graham on a pedestal.

If I were to talk to Billy Graham, however, he would most likely give Jesus all the credit for anything good that came from his life. While we may often be tempted to exalt those who have made a positive impact on our lives, or even those we read about in the pages of the Bible, it is not God's intention that we do so. Jesus is the only man who walked the earth and is worthy of such veneration. Everyone else, no matter how faithful and admirable, is still merely a man created in God's image who has fallen short of His glory.

God doesn't really need us: we are not necessary to the spreading of the Gospel, or the furtherance of His kingdom, or the teaching of His Word. God is perfectly able in His omnipotence to accomplish such tasks on His own. He is, however, a Father who loves to include His children in the work of His kingdom. Therefore, He tasks us with missions and gifts us with abilities to join in with what He is doing all around us. Ultimately, the glory goes to Him for the great things He has done, is doing, and will do.

When man seems so honorable and we're tempted to lift him up, we must be careful to give all the credit to the One who makes it all possible: Jesus

When do you look to man instead of recognizing the One who is behind the man?

_____

_____

How do you tend to place people on pedestals when Jesus is the only One who deserves such an honor?

_____

_____

In the future, what steps can you take to protect yourself from such man-worship?

_____

_____

Heavenly Father,

I praise You for being the Maker of Heaven and earth and for all the amazing godly influences You have placed in my life. I admit I sometimes think there is something saint-like about these important people and I often lift them to a higher place than they deserve. Help me to see that Jesus is the One who deserves such admiration. May I always worship You as the only One worthy of my adoration.

In Jesus' Name I pray, Amen

52 Days of Faith

8

Master of the House

"'Moses was faithful as a servant in all God's house,' bearing witness to what would be spoken by God in the future. But Christ is faithful as the Son over God's house. And we are his house, if indeed we hold firmly to our confidence and the hope in which we glory" (Hebrews 3:5-6).

"It's backwards," I commented as I turned on the wrong light for what seemed like the hundredth time that day. "The electrician should have wired the switches to correspond to the position of the light. This layout doesn't make sense." There were several things that didn't add up in our new house, like the phone jack located in the family room while the cable TV outlet was in the kitchen or the patio sloping down toward the house, so water pooled by the back door when it rained. As the homeowner, I didn't have any control over how the builder constructed my house.

In the same way that my house reflects the thought and care the designer put into its construction, so it is with the people of God through faith in Jesus Christ. As the master of the house of God, the church, Jesus is faithful. Therefore, we can trust Him as we embark on this grand adventure of life, knowing that whatever we face is already overcome. We can place our hope in Him because He will never let us down. We have everything to look forward to because He is preparing a place for us that will far outshine our every expectation.

Minister James Melvin Washington said, "My grandmother used to tell me that every boss is temporary, that every rainy day is temporary, that every hardship is temporary. She used to tell me, 'Son, every good-bye ain't gone. Just hold on— there's joy coming in the morning.'" While a nice sentiment, it wouldn't mean anything if our hope is not rooted in something. Without Christ, our hope that there is something better to come is a pie-in-the-sky kind of foolish wish. In Christ, however, this hope is based on a firm foundation. In Christ, we can have confidence that the Master of our house has a plan that brings joy untold.

Do you live your life as if there is no master plan,
despairing at heartache and pain
like it's all for naught?

_____

_____

When are you afraid of what is to come?
How can you encourage yourself and others to trust in
Jesus with day-to-day struggles?

_____

_____

Heavenly Father,

I admit I often forget the good and beneficial plan You have for my life. I often despair when things go wrong, wondering what good could come out of it. Help me to trust Jesus as the Master of my life, knowing with confidence that what is to come is far better than I could ever imagine. Give me more faith to be able to see things from Your perspective. May my heart be inclined toward You this day.

In Jesus' Name I pray, Amen

9

Profile of a Hardened Heart

"So, as the Holy Spirit says; 'Today, if you hear his voice, do not harden your hearts as you did in the rebellion, during the time of testing in the wilderness, where your ancestors tested and tried me, though for forty years they saw what I did. That is why I was angry with that generation; I said, "Their hearts are always going astray, and they have not known my ways." So I declared an oath in my anger, "They shall never enter my rest."'

See to it, brothers and sisters, that none of you has a sinful, unbelieving heart that turns away from the living God. But encourage one another daily, as long as it is called 'Today,' so that none of you may be hardened by sin's deceitfulness. We have come to share in Christ, if indeed we hold our original conviction firmly to the very end. As has just been said: 'Today, if you hear his voice, do not harden your hearts as you did in the rebellion'" (Hebrews 3:7-15).

I never go hungry, or naked, or without shelter. I am surrounded by a family who loves me and friends who care. My every need is supplied, many wants are granted, and some dreams are fulfilled. The beauty of creation that is all around me takes my breath away. Still, it's easy to forget the One who makes all this possible.

A friend of mine recently recounted an experience at her part-time job when a distraught woman entered the consignment shop where she works on an intermittent basis. After a few minutes of visiting, the customer began to open up about her woes, describing a heart-wrenching series of events that would leave even the most faithful feeling distraught. Miraculously, my friend was in a very similar situation years ago and was able to comfort her with the very comfort she had received from the God of compassion. Even more incredible was the fact that even though the store had been very busy the hour before, as soon as this hurting soul entered the shop, not one customer interrupted their impromptu counseling session.

How easy it is to chalk up as pure happenstance such mind-blowing choreography of the intricate lives of so many in order to orchestrate such a meeting. Or to simply not notice how God lovingly arranged for the opportunity. Or to take such a mighty work for granted, failing to praise Him for His sovereignty and attention to detail.

Our hearts are hardened in many ways, just like the Israelites who tasted the manna, drank from bitter water-turned-sweet, and wore clothing that never faded nor deteriorated. Still, they failed to recognize His faithful provision, His uncanny foresight, or His powerful protection. Instead, they trained their attentions upon what they missed, or how things could be better, or the difficulty of their circumstances.

Let us develop eyes to see all the intricate patterns He is weaving into the tapestry of our lives. May we choose to look for all the good He has provided instead of all the bad that can overwhelm. Might we look for ways to give God praise in the big and small things of each day. In this way, we will guard against developing an unbelieving heart that quickly strays away from the living God.

It only takes a heartache to turn my heart away,
When all He really wants from me is to trust Him
through the fray.

How do you fail to see all the ways God takes care of you, big and small?

_____

_____

When do you take credit for something God orchestrated? Why do you think God continues to supply our needs, even when we don't acknowledge Him?

_____

_____

Heavenly Father,

I praise You for how You faithfully supply for my needs and pay attention to the countless details of my life. I fail to give You credit for much of what You do, putting me in danger of developing a hard heart. Please give me eyes to see Your faithful provision, and a heart to acknowledge all Your mighty ways. It is my intention to wholeheartedly confess my need for You each moment of every day. I praise You for Your loving care.
In Jesus' name I pray, Amen

10
Danger of Unbelief

"Who were they who heard and rebelled? Were they not all those Moses led out of Egypt? And with whom was he angry for forty years? Was it not with those who sinned, whose bodies perished in the wilderness? And to whom did God swear that they would never enter his rest if not to those who disobeyed? So we see that they were not able to enter, because of their unbelief" (Hebrews 3:16-19).

I often look at the news and bristle at the evil behind all the wicked events taking place in the world today. I wonder about the hearts of the people responsible for such malevolence and imagine God's wrath as He brings down justice upon them for all the suffering they have caused. It's easy to see how they deserve punishment.

What about those who have professed a faith in Jesus Christ? Do we ever anger God? Does He ever have to go to great lengths to discipline us? Are we in danger of losing His blessing in any way? God is unbelievably patient. He is abundantly loving. His mercies are bottomless, fresh every morning. Yet God is also perfectly just and righteous.

Consequently, while the blood of Jesus saves us from God's condemnation, does it protect us from a falling-out of the usual intimacy with Him, or His rod of correction, or His pruning shears? As His children, we are expected to trust Him to lead, teach, provide and fulfill. Yet, we often go astray, as the Israelites did, forgetting His mighty acts of salvation and focusing only on the threat at hand, or doubting His ability to provide, or are unwilling to take God's omnipotent, sovereign nature into account. We are just as rebellious as the Israelites in many ways. Can we expect God to look the other way in the face of such unbelief? Are we really shielded from God's righteous anger because we belong to Him? To answer simply, God does not play favorites (Romans 2:1-11).

This is not to say the blood of Jesus does not protect us from eternal damnation --it does. But God makes it clear throughout scripture that He is focused on the hearts of His people. Therefore, we must pay attention to our tendency to grow cold-hearted against the suffering we see all around us. It is important to stay connected to Him, seeing God as our Father who is the only source of our provision instead of conforming to the world's ways of selfish pursuits. He cares about our willingness to cooperate with His indwelling Spirit instead of going back to our old ways of letting our fleshly lusts rule.

It is not just the darkness in this world that God detests. That is obviously evil. It is also the unbelief of His children by faith that causes a rift between us and our Father. He made the ultimate sacrifice to repair our relationship, and He desires that we trust Him in every way. Let's not try His patience because of our stubborn insistence on living independently from Him. Instead, we can taste the abundant life Jesus came to deliver simply by resting in His perfect provision, protection, and purpose.

How often we walk in uncertainty,
the Shepherd hard to see
but His staff is right beside us
If only we'd believe.

How do you assume you're safe from God's anger and rebel against Him, hoping He'll turn a blind eye?

_____

_____

When do you neglect to include your Father in every decision you make?

_____

_____

How would your life change if you realized God's desire for you to trust Him completely?

_____

_____

Heavenly Father,

I know I have angered You many times with my unwillingness to obey, my determined independence or my insistence on going after my own needs. How often I have gone off on my own, stubbornly trying to make a go of my life apart from You. I realize how much You love me and how deeply You desire my constant company and confidence. Help me to turn away from rebellion, choosing instead to trust You fully.
In Jesus' Name I pray, Amen

11

Enter His Rest

"There remains, then, a Sabbath-rest for the people of God; for anyone who enters God's rest also rests from their works, just as God did from his. Let us, therefore, make every effort to enter that rest, so that no one will perish by following their example of disobedience" (Hebrews 4:9-11).

It didn't sound like it would work for us. When my husband and I looked at the pile of wood and hardware laying before us on the floor, and we compared that to the directions on how to put the pieces together to make a bookshelf, we decided our idea was better than the detailed plan that was presented in the instructions. It seemed too complicated and hard to follow, so we set off on our own, determined to complete the bookcase in no time at all.

Several frustrating hours later, as we were trying in vain to place the molding, the finishing piece broke off. Now every time I look at that bookcase with the cracked molding, I remember how we foolishly chose our way instead of taking advantage of the work the builder had done beforehand in writing the directions.

In the same way the creator of that bookshelf knew how it needed to be put together to achieve the best possible outcome, and carefully thought through how best to package his product for our benefit, God as our Creator and Author of our story did all the work necessary for us to walk the path that leads to life. When we accept the teaching, rebuking, correcting, and training in righteousness that His Word delivers, we are equipped to live as He intended, thus reflecting well on Him.

When we enter into a relationship with God through faith in Jesus Christ, we receive the benefit of His indwelling Spirit who guides and empowers us to live through Him. Unfortunately, all too often we choose to go against His teaching, deny His guidance, and rebel against His ways. In short, we try to find our own way to what Jesus has already sacrificed to deliver; the hope of life eternal and peace with God.

The foundation of the Gospel of Jesus Christ is grace. We receive salvation as a gift of God. Even though our identity in Christ is permanently secured by His blood, it's easy to try to earn what was freely given to us. We can confuse God's desire for us to follow Him with an expectation that we try hard to do as He says in order to earn our keep or stay in His good graces. Instead, Jesus already did all the work that was necessary to secure our justification and atonement for sins when He died on the cross. Now we, as His inheritance by faith, can rest. He did the work, we do the resting.

We enter into His rest when we cooperate with the work the Spirit is doing to transform us into the image of Christ. We enter into His rest when we realize His Word is a living and active tool used to shape us into the men and women He created us to be, not simply an instruction manual for us to follow. We enter into His rest when we allow Him to have His way as our Shepherd, forsaking the lure of our fleshly desires. And most of all, we enter into His rest when we simply enjoy His presence throughout our days. God did all the work, we can enter into His rest through faith in Jesus Christ.

God gave His Son, Jesus gave His life, the Holy Spirit gave Himself so that we can live in relationship with Him. Stubbornly forgetting how much has been done on our behalf and insisting on working to earn the life we've already been given denies God's best for us: His rest.

Won't you stop working to earn what has already been given, to accomplish what has previously been finished, to transform yourself when it's a work of God's hand? Won't you enter into God's rest?

How do you work hard to earn what God has already freely given through faith in Jesus Christ?

_____

_____

When are you hesitant to receive God's best for you, thinking you somehow have to make an effort to contribute?

_____

_____

In which part of your life are you stubbornly sticking to your guns instead of willingly submitting to God's transforming work in your life?

_____

_____

Heavenly Father,

I praise You for Your gracious gift of salvation and the abundant life that follows. Even though You've already done everything that was necessary to secure my place in Your kingdom, I admit I feel guilty being on the receiving end. Help me to accept what You have done for me and enter into Your rest. Give me the faith to believe You have accomplished all that is necessary so that I can submit to Your plan, willingly allowing You to change me into the person You created me to be. I trust in You to do all the work and desire to become like pliable clay in Your hands.

In Jesus' Name I pray, Amen

12

There's No Fooling God

"Let us, therefore, make every effort to enter that rest, so that no one will perish by following their example of disobedience. For the word of God is alive and active. Sharper than any double-edged sword, it penetrates even to dividing soul and spirit, joints and marrow; it judges the thoughts and attitudes of the heart. Nothing in all creation is hidden from God's sight. Everything is uncovered and laid bare before the eyes of him to whom we must give account" (Hebrews 4:11-13).

I wanted to go home. We were out of money, almost out of gas, and tired of traveling. All I wanted to do was hunker down in a familiar place and rest. The problem was, we had no home to go back to. My husband and I were traveling cross-country in a rented moving truck, driving down a deserted highway in a remote area of Wyoming. The rest of our family of six followed behind in our two vehicles. Instead of staying put until the delayed income hit our account, we were continuing forward in faith. I suddenly felt foolish and reckless and wanted to forget about this move across the country and simply give up and go back to our life on the east coast. The problem was, God was calling us west.

We all face times in our lives when we just want to go back to where things were comfortable, where we knew where our next meal was coming from, where we understood how things worked. When walking by faith, however, it's necessary to trust God to provide without panicking at the current lack. It's also crucial to acknowledge God's power and His ability to provide, protect and lead. Faith also means we'll have to get as comfortable with the unknown as we are with the known.

We can try to fake this faith, moving forward as if we're trusting God, but as soon as we come into contact with God's Word, the fear, doubt, and disbelief rooted in our heart will be exposed. People may think we are looking to God to provide, but the Bible will convict us of the anxiety hidden deep within. We can tell ourselves God can do anything, but His Word will show us how small we've actually made Him. Even if we never utter a word of complaint, the Holy Scripture uncovers a sense of impatience found within us of the mysterious nature of God's plan.

We can't hide the true state of our heart from God and His Word. Martin Luther, father of the Reformation, knew this all too well. He said, "The Bible is alive, it speaks to me; it has feet, it runs after me; it has hands, it lays hold of me." There's no hiding when it comes to Scripture. Therefore, we would be wise to expose ourselves to God's Word often, as uncomfortable as that may be. We will never be sorry for spending time developing such a worthy habit.

God's Word is more than a book.
It is a tool God uses to expose the true state of our hearts.

How do you bluff your way through your relationship with God, pretending to walk by faith when fear really rules your heart?

_____

_____

How much time do you spend in God's Word?

_____

_____

When you do, is it with an open heart so that God can work, or do you just read so you can check another task off your list?

_____

_____

Heavenly Father,
I admit I often go through the motions, trying to bluff my way through life. I know I need Your Word to show me where I'm off and convict me of my wrong attitudes. Help me to open myself up to Your living, active Word, becoming a pliable lump of clay in Your loving hands.

Give me a hunger for Your Word, for I know it will change my life like no other book can.
In Jesus' Name I pray, Amen

13

Jesus Gets It

"Therefore, since we have a great high priest who has ascended into heaven, Jesus the Son of God, let us hold firmly to the faith we profess. For we do not have a high priest who is unable to empathize with our weaknesses, but we have one who has been tempted in every way, just as we are—yet he did not sin. Let us then approach God's throne of grace with confidence, so that we may receive mercy and find grace to help us in our time of need" (Hebrews 4:14-160).

It's easy to think no one will understand, that we're the only one who has withstood such pressure, or faced such suffering, or been plagued by such strong impulses. While our enemy would like us to think we're all alone in our peculiar temptations, giving us the idea that we must keep our struggles in the dark, nothing could be further from the truth. We have a Friend who empathizes and is therefore approachable.

Jesus is the only one who truly understands the strength of temptation. He fully knows the weight of attraction that comes with a craving, desire or compulsion. Only Jesus comprehends how hard it is to resist sin. How is this? Jesus understands our battle against living in sin because He faithfully and perfectly resisted temptation. Only in successfully standing strong against an attack does one fully know the power of his enemy. Such is the case with

Jesus and sin. Since He never gave in, He knows the full potency of temptation. Never having succumbed to its enticements, He held up under its pressure, fully bearing its weight.

This means we have a compassionate ally when it comes to resisting the lure of sins that are so appealing to our nature. Even if no one around us gets why it's so hard for us to stay away from what tempts us, Jesus does. And this is not all. Since He is our perfect Priest, flawless Mediator, and empathetic Intercessor, Jesus makes it possible for us to receive the grace and mercy we need to stand up under temptation. And, we receive these necessary tools straight from the Source. We don't have to cower in shame, lurk in the shadows out of embarrassment or disgrace, nor stay where we are out of guilty resignation. Instead, we have been given a way out, an opportunity to rise up out of the muck, and in fact have a Great High Priest who reaches down to pull us out.

Won't you take His hand this day, the High Priest who makes victory over sin possible?

How do you feel like a victim when it comes to sin? Are you powerless against its lure?

_____

_____

Do you realize the benefit you have in Christ when it comes to resisting temptation?

_____

_____

How can you take advantage of such a weapon against sin?

_____

_____

Heavenly Father,

Sometimes my sin does make me feel guilty and shameful. I do tend to hide those parts from You, thinking there is no one who would understand or be able to help me. I now know that Jesus is the One who can understand how hard it is for me, but also empowers me to overcome the sin that so easily entangles me. I am not without defense when it comes to sin. Hallelujah! I am not destined to live as I always have. Through Christ, I have a way out. Thank You for making victory over sin possible. In Jesus' Name I pray, Amen

52 Days of Faith

14

The Pain of Obedience

"Son though he was, he learned obedience from what he suffered" (Hebrews 5:8).

He was no superman. He wasn't born with under-standing and perfection. Jesus came into this world as a genuine human being, setting aside His divine rights for a time so that He could become man. Therefore, as He grew, He was faced with every-thing the average person encounters in life. It was only in meeting the temptation to disobey, the lure of the flesh, and the pull of pride did He prove His obedience, purity, and humility. These qualities came about as He learned them naturally, like any child does. The only difference is that He never failed to comply, never gave into sinful tendencies, and never succumbed to self-centered behavior.

This changes everything for us as followers of Christ. Not only does He get it, understanding the difficulties of living in this world, but He is a God who knows how to learn. He gained practice in obedience by doing it. It wasn't something that came naturally to Him as a fleshly man, but He attained it by doing as His Father bid.

When Jesus prayed in agony in the Garden of Gethsemane before He faced the cross, He asked His Father to remove this calling from His life. His flesh pleaded for Him to avoid such suffering at all costs. There is no greater picture of the natural man meeting His divine nature. As His Son, He wanted His Father's will above all things, but as a man, He knew what it would cost Him (Matthew 26:39). Yet, He obeyed. He willingly laid down His life so that we could live (John 10:18).

We need not be discouraged by Jesus' example of righteous living. He was God, so how can we relate. Even though He is God's Son, He did not possess special powers that enabled Him to always do the right thing. Instead, He had to practice obedience just like we do. He felt the pain in giving up His right to Himself, in denying His fleshly desires, in choosing His Father's will over His own. Therefore, we can draw much inspiration from His example as well as power to follow in His footsteps. Obedience is what sanctifies us, so we must take it seriously. As the early-20th Century Chinese Christian leader and teacher, Watchman Nee said, "To what are we consecrated? Not to Christian work, but to the will of God, to be and to do whatever he requires."

Jesus had to learn obedience,
so I must follow suit.
Doing as God says will not be convenient,
As I let Him choose my route.

How do you tend to think it's impossible to obey God so you don't even try?

_____

_____

When could you gain strength from thinking of Christ's struggle as He set His mind to obey despite the discomfort His compliance would cause?

_____

_____

How does Jesus give you hope?

_____

_____

Heavenly Father,
I thank You for sending Jesus to make a way for me to get to You. As I walk with You, I often find it difficult to give up my own desires so I can follow Yours. Seeing how much Jesus struggled to obey You, I realize it's not an easy thing to submit. Help me to make such a commitment to do as You say that I would be willing to sweat drops of blood as Jesus did in my struggle to obey.
In Jesus' Name I pray, Amen

15

The Superior Priest

"During the days of Jesus' life on earth, he offered up prayers and petitions with fervent cries and tears to the one who could save him from death, and he was heard because of his reverent submission. Son though he was, he learned obedience from what he suffered and, once made perfect, he became the source of eternal salvation for all who obey him and was designated by God to be high priest in the order of Melchizedek" (Hebrews 5:7-10).

Sacrifice was always necessary. At first, it was up to each person to offer their own sacrifices before God. Then, starting with Noah, the rite was taken up by the head of each family (Genesis 8:20). Later, as the nation of Israel came into being, God instituted a priestly line through the tribe of Levi to continue this vital ritual. Why? Because without a blood sacrifice, forgiveness from God for the sins of mankind is not possible.

If this is such an important ceremony, why do we fail to offer up animals on an altar to God in order to receive atonement for our sins? This ancient rite is no longer necessary because a perfect sacrifice was made by a rare man who was both King and Priest. While all other priests, save one, could be distinguished by their Levitical lineage, this priest stunned us all by showing up in a mysterious way that caused many to doubt His authority and position. How could such an important title be filled by an obscure carpenter's son, born of a virgin, who came from Nazareth?

There once was a similar king and priest in Abram's time. This king of Salem blessed Abram, generously serving a meal of bread and wine. By faith, Abram honored this man's authority and position as a designation from God Himself by giving him a tenth of everything (Genesis 14:18-20). Is this not how we must receive Jesus? It is only by faith that we believe and are then saved by His perfect, powerful and eternal sacrifice. Even though He did not come through the line of Levi, as prescribed by God in order to serve as priest and offer sacrifices, He has the unique distinction of being designated directly by God to serve as our eternal and perfect High Priest, as well as our righteous King of peace whose reign cannot be disturbed.

Through Christ, our Priest who is superior in every way, we can be firmly established in the family of God as children whose sins are completely covered. We are forever forgiven.

All it takes to receive such a pardon is the faith to believe He is who He says He is and submit accordingly.

We have a great High Priest, Jesus Christ, who came into the world as the Son of God, lived a sinless life, offered himself as a perfect sacrifice for the sins of his

people, rose to everlasting life at the right hand of the majesty of God, and there loves us and prays for us and bids us draw near to God through him.
—John Piper.

How do you struggle to trust your life to Jesus, doubting whether He is really the Son of God who came to take away the sins of the world?

_____

_____

When do you fail to take Jesus at His Word, fully accepting Him as He is presented in Scripture, preferring instead to receive a more pop-culture version of Him?

_____

_____

Since Jesus is King and Priest, He completely fulfills all your needs. Won't you trust Him fully today?

_____

_____

Heavenly Father,
I admit I sometimes dilute the character of Jesus, making Him to be less than what He is. In reality, He's

perfectly chosen to serve as my King and Priest, ruling compassionately and rightly while offering Himself as the final, flawless sacrifice that would forever atone for my sins. Help me to trust in Him fully, accepting Him by faith in the same way that Abram recognized Melchizedek as a special kind of priest.

In Jesus' Name I pray, Amen

16
It's Not All in Your Head

"We have much to say about this, but it is hard to make it clear to you because you no longer try to understand. In fact, though by this time you ought to be teachers, you need someone to teach you the elementary truths of God's word all over again. You need milk, not solid food! Anyone who lives on milk, being still an infant, is not acquainted with the teaching about righteousness. But solid food is for the mature, who by constant use have trained themselves to distinguish good from evil" (Hebrews 5:11-14).

She was an expert in her field. People would come from miles around to ask her questions about marriage and seek marital counseling. Her knowledge was beyond compare. Still, her relationship with her own husband lacked intimacy and mutual respect. Due to her unwillingness to practice what she made a living preaching, her own marriage suffered.

Reading God's Word is good. Learning more about God and His ways is vital to our growth as believers. We all need to spend time meditating on the truths found in the Bible. But if all that knowledge just stays in our heads and is never put to use, never tested, never tried, what good is it? It remains a concept, an idea or a theory, never believed enough to be put into practice.

This is how we get into trouble as followers of Christ. We float along, depending on what little knowledge we have and thinking of ourselves as Christians but never really living it out. Then comes a teacher whose words sound so good that we fall in behind them, swallowing their lessons without question, never comparing it to what is being taught in God's Word. Or we enter a time of trial and find our faith is hollow, nothing more than empty words that sounded good but give us nothing solid on which to stand. Or something better comes along, and we succumb to the lure of the things of this world, leaving behind that which was meant to perfectly sustain and fulfill, but was never cultivated so that we could taste the abundant life Jesus promised (John 10:10).

It's like the college graduate who earned a master's degree in business but has never put his knowledge into practice. His background looks good on paper until he tries to start up a company and is clueless as to where to start. He studied for years to gain the accreditation, but it does him no good if he can't apply the knowledge to real life. This is why internships can be such a valuable tool in our education; to give us a chance to use what we've learned.

Similarly, this walk with Jesus consists of much on-the-job training. Book knowledge is fine, but it does no good if we can't put it into practice. So, it's time to stop simply learning and start training, trying out what we know to be true.

If all we do is learn about Jesus
But never take Him at His Word
Are we walking with Him
Or simply watching from the sidelines?

Are you putting what you learn from God's Word into practice, or only living out your faith in your head?

_____

_____

Do you find it hard to see the truth played out in front of you, never really applying what you read in the Bible to your current situation?

_____

_____

How can you start cultivating a responsive heart that is moved to action by what you read?

_____

_____

Heavenly Father,
   I admit that I often fail to put into practice the truths You teach me in Your Word into practice. Help me to trust You enough to do what You say, not simply agree with

You in theory. Give me more faith to be able to walk with You through all the storms of life, holding onto Your hand as You lead me down difficult paths. It's time for me to leave the milk behind and move onto something more substantial. It's time for me to live out my faith.
In Jesus Name I pray, Amen.

17
Spoon-Fed

"We have much to say about this, but it is hard to make it clear to you because you no longer try to understand. In fact, though by this time you ought to be teachers, you need someone to teach you the elementary truths of God's word all over again. Anyone who lives on milk, being still an infant, is not acquainted with the teaching about righteousness. But solid food is for the mature, who by constant use have trained themselves to distinguish good from evil" (Hebrews 5:11-14).

I remember the special times I shared with my firstborn daughter, feeding her as she sat in her high chair. I can picture how some of the pureed food would dribble down her chin. I would then use the spoon to scoop it up and give it another go, placing the nourishment again in her open mouth, hoping it goes down to her stomach this time. All my daughter had to do to satisfy her hunger was close her lips down over the spoon and swallow what was given to her. As much as I enjoyed this time, I have to admit I was glad when she was able to feed herself.

It's the same with the Word of God. I don't mind teaching truths to a new believer, breaking down scripture passages and gleaning the meaning from the text. In essence, I'm spoon-feeding them the Word of God. At some point, though, I expect that they will be able to feed themselves, digging through scripture on their own, listening to the teaching of the Holy Spirit within as He reveals nuggets of truth in each passage.

Milk is meant to nourish us until we are ready for solid food. It's transitory in nature, not meant to be permanent. Therefore, let us strive to move forward, developing our own hunger for God's Word and the life-transformation found within its pages. To our encouragement, our ability to understand His Word is not dependent upon our intelligence, our study skills, or our education level. Instead, it is only determined by our willingness to listen to what God is saying, our sensitivity to His leading, and our desire to know Him better.

God's Word is not like any other book. It's not like the textbooks that were required reading in school, or like an instruction manual that we must memorize and adhere to. Instead, it is living and active. The Bible is alive and breathing, able to accomplish in and of itself the things God intends to achieve through His own Word (Isaiah 55:9-11). Like Evangelist John Stott exhorts us, "We must allow the Word of God to confront us, to disturb our security, to undermine our complacency and to overthrow our patterns of thought and behavior." Scripture is powerful in and of itself. The only variable, then, is us. Are we attentive, compliant, and pliable readers of God's Word, or do we expect to be spoon-fed?

If you have the Spirit without the Word,
you blow up.
If you have the Word without the Spirit,
you dry up
If you have both the Word and the Spirit,
you grow up.
—Don Lyon

How are you waiting for someone else to teach you God's Word instead of opening it up yourself?

_____

_____

When are you intimidated by the Bible?

_____

_____

How can you take a step today to trust God and His Word enough to start studying the Bible for yourself?

_____

_____

Heavenly Father,

I believe that Your Word is living and active, able to teach me truth, show me where I'm wrong, train me to live rightly, and equip me for the work You've created for me to do. Give me courage, then, to open the Bible and read it for myself, and give me the sensitivity to detect Your leading and the confidence to trust Your teaching. I believe You will use Your own Word to change my life; may I be like pliable clay in Your loving hands.
In Jesus' Name I pray, Amen

18

There's No Going Back

"It is impossible for those who have once been enlightened, who have tasted the heavenly gift, who have shared in the Holy Spirit, who have tasted the goodness of the word of God and the powers of the coming age and who have fallen away, to be brought back to repentance. To their loss they are crucifying the Son of God all over again and subjecting Him to public disgrace. Land that drinks in the rain often falling on it and that produces a crop useful to those for whom it is farmed receives the blessing of God. But land that produces thorns and thistles is worthless and is in danger of being cursed. In the end it will be burned" (Hebrews 6:4-8).

This may be one of the strongest warnings against apostasy, counterfeit conversion and Christian religiosity in all of scripture. The time in which we live is filled with such deception as to lead many away from the core truth of the Gospel, fooling them into believing they are saved and headed to Heaven when in fact they are not. Paul warns for this very reason that we should "Examine (ourselves) to see whether (we) are in the faith; test (ourselves)" (2 Corinthians 13:5). In other words, instead of spending time evaluating the faith of others, we must consider whether we ourselves are living our lives as committed believers in Jesus Christ because our eternal welfare is at stake.

After all, He gave His very life so that we might live. He sacrificed His divine rights for a time in order to deliver salvation to us. He endured excruciating suffering out of obedience to His Father whose heart broke at our estrangement from Him. He became sin, even though sinless and without the common human experience of giving in to temptation, so that we can take on His righteousness and have all the benefits of a rightful heir of God.

Jesus accomplished much on our behalf. He gave up everything for us. How, then, can we take His sacrifice lightly? The truth is, if we truly belong to Christ, are bought by His blood and have surrendered fully to His lordship, we will not. We will recognize we were bought with a price and will increasingly appreciate more and more the steep price paid to redeem us from the pit of Hell.

And the joyful reality is, there is no going back. Once we belong to Jesus, we're His forever. On the flip side, however, is a sobering truth. If we reject Jesus Christ even though we see our need for Him, there is no second chance for us. If we discard Him like yesterday's leftovers despite the fact we've witnessed the fruit of His Word and saw glimpses of the goodness of God at work in our lives, there is no second chance for us. If we refuse to turn away from selfish living and place Jesus on the throne of our life in the face of the realization of His graciousness in waiting for us to come around, then there is no second chance for us. If we reject His offer of life eternal even though we've been convicted in our heart of the reality of Hell and the absolute wonder of Heaven, then there is no second chance for us. And only the Lord knows when we've crossed that point of no return.

We must remember if we make the choice to turn away from all the goodness we've tasted in Christ, we can't change our minds later and enter into the fold. We've selected our side and now we're on the outside looking in-- permanently. A true disciple of Christ, however, is unable to turn away from Him if truly enlightened to His Lordship and submitted to His sovereign rule. In other words, if you truly belong to Him, you are His forever, your fate sealed with the down payment of the Holy Spirit living within (2 Corinthians 1:21-22).

This is not to say as believers we can't experience periods of doubt, or lack of faith, or times of questioning. No, this is addressing the practice of tasting and seeing that the Lord is good, then choosing to live a life of perversity, or to speak out against Jesus Christ, or to write Him off as unnecessary. These kinds of public, intentional, complete rejections of a faith once considered are very difficult to be taken back.

The death of Jesus, one man, was enough to save all of mankind. In the same way, our acceptance of Him as Lord and Savior is a one-time deal. If His free gift of salvation through faith is rejected once perceived, it may no longer be an offer that is on the table. Therefore, if you hear His voice calling you, do not harden your hearts (Hebrews 3:7-8) but respond and give your lives to Him for it may be your only chance. As Dr. Steven Lawson of One Passion Ministries said, "Hell is full of sincere, religious people, never born again, and Heaven is full of immoral people who repented and believed in Christ." Make sure you know to which group you belong.

> *Love was shown when Jesus died*
> *'Twas not an easy cost applied*
> *Yet when I consider entering His fold*
> *I can't expect to come and go.*

How do you risk turning away from God by taking lightly Jesus' sacrifice? Are you absolutely sure you belong to Christ?

_____

_____

What evidence do you see that you are growing closer to Jesus every day?"

_____

_____

Do you cherish Jesus as He is meant to be treasured?

_____

_____

Heavenly Father,

My place in your family is secure since Your love for me cannot be lost. I pray that I will always be devoted to You, taking the sacrifice Jesus made as fully appreciated and necessary for my salvation. May I never take that for granted. Help me to cling to You as my sole source of all good things and my greatest treasure. I admit I often stray, turning toward my own fleshly desires as if they were more important. It is my desire that I would keep You at the center of my attentions, wanting nothing more than what You lavishly give me. I'm so thankful for Jesus who makes our relationship possible.

In Jesus' Name I pray, Amen

52 Days of Faith

19

God Doesn't Miss a Thing

"Even though we speak like this, dear friends, we are convinced of better things in your case—the things that have to do with salvation. God is not unjust; he will not forget your work and the love you have shown him as you have helped his people and continued to help them. We want each of you to show this same diligence to the very end, so that what you hope for may be fully realized. We do not want you to become lazy, but to imitate those who through faith and patience inherit what has been promised" (Hebrews 6:9-12).

It's easy to grow indifferent, apathetic, and un-concerned. Even though the very Spirit of God lives within us through faith in Jesus Christ, propelling us to love the unlovable, care for our brothers and sisters, and bear with one another in love. We live in an uncaring and cold world. Every day we are bombarded with examples of cruelty toward the helpless, a survival-of-the-fittest mentality, an every-man-for-himself way of living. We see examples played out in front of us of how to give up on those who can't seem to get their act together. Divorce, law suits, and child neglect show how quick man is to quit on one another.

Our flesh is so easily drawn to such an approach. Therefore, it is vital that we keep on pushing for-ward, striving diligently toward the finish line. Even if it seems no one notices how we live out God's love, He sees every sacrifice, each baby step, all the ways we pour out His love to a hurting world.

There was once a woman who was hurting deeply. Her physical ailment sent her to every kind of medical expert who promised healing but never delivered. In desperation, she recklessly reached out to Jesus in her unclean state, hoping that He would be the one who would finally give her freedom from her suffering. As soon as she touched the hem of His garment, she was made whole; the bleeding which had been part of her life for twelve long years suddenly stopped. Jesus knew the moment the healing power left Him, aware that someone had benefited from the supernatural force that flowed through Him from the Father (Luke 8:43-48).

It is the same with us. We have the power of God flowing through us by faith in Jesus Christ. We are not able to love apart from Jesus. We cannot care for those who are hurting without the compassion of Christ compelling us to do such an unnatural thing. It is impossible to keep on ministering to the flock without the living waters bubbling up from an eternal spring inside of us. Everything we do by the power of the indwelling Holy Spirit is noticed by God. He is perfectly aware of how His power is being used throughout all of creation to tend to His image-bearers. He does not miss a thing.

If the faith we have in Jesus Christ is truly ours, we will discover a desire to do things that go against our natural tendencies, to accomplish what is impossible, and to carry on in the midst of harassment. If, however, this faith is more of a religion, something we take part in because it makes us feel good and we know it's good for us, there will be no strength to endure, no ability to do what is difficult, and no reason to persevere. As James Black said, "Borrowed beliefs have no power."

We must, then, cling to Jesus, depending on Him to drive us forward with the hope that all our efforts are not in vain. Continuing on even when it seems our labors mean nothing, our hard work has gone unnoticed, or the pains we take to carry on do not make a difference, shows that our faith is real. We must not grow weary of doing what we are called to do, letting the world's indifferent attitude become our own. God does not overlook any effort that is made through His power. He is perfectly aware of our faithfulness, and is ready to deliver on His promise when the time comes.

Don't grow tired of doing God's bidding because nothing done through Jesus is in vain.

How do you feel like giving up because it seems your work is not making a difference?

_____

_____

When do you look for results instead of just focusing on pleasing God in your obedience?

_____

_____

How are you in danger of becoming cold and indifferent?

_____

_____

Heavenly Father,

I am so thankful for Your willingness to send Your Son to die for me. Through Jesus, I have the ability to do amazing things in this cold and heartless world. Still, I often am tempted to give up, wondering if an impact is being made. Help me to stay true to You, desiring to please You in all I do as I realize my efforts do not pass by You unnoticed. You are perfectly aware of how Your power is being used throughout Your creation. May I always strive to be an instrument of Your love in a world that desperately needs such compassion.

In Jesus' Name I pray, Amen

20
It's Just a Matter of Time

**"People swear by someone greater than them-
selves, and the oath confirms what is said and puts
an end to all argument. Because God wanted to
make the unchanging nature of his purpose very
clear to the heirs of what was promised, he
confirmed it with an oath. God did this so that, by
two unchangeable things in which it is impossible
for God to lie, we who have fled to take hold of the
hope set before us may be greatly encouraged. We
have this hope as an anchor for the soul, firm and
secure. It enters the inner sanctuary behind the
curtain, where our forerunner, Jesus, has entered
on our behalf. He has become a high priest forever,
in the order of Melchizedek" (Hebrews 6:16-20).**

We see it all the time, especially in the world of
politics. Something changes, things go differently
than expected, the meticulously-crafted house of
cards starts to crumble, and the lies begin. Rarely
does a leader take responsibility for his or her
decisions. Instead, others are blamed, history is re-
written, and the public relations machine whirrs into
action to perform damage control.

This is why we have a hard time believing people
at their word. Even for those who mean well and
honestly intend to deliver on a promise, life happens
and their inability to control circumstances results in
them not doing as they said they would do. For

instance, a parent reassures his child by saying, "Don't worry, I will always be here for you." Then the accident happens, the unexpected illness strikes, or the divorce is finalized. Suddenly, the man is not there for his son like he had wanted to be. This wounded boy then grows up angry and disillusioned, unable to trust anyone since his father let him down.

God is not in this same boat. He is unable to deceive, saying something just to placate us or believing at the time the promise is given He will come through only to change His mind in the end. Neither is He at the mercy of anything at all. Instead, He is above all things and is completely in control, sovereign over all His creation. For this reason, He is the only One who is capable to deliver on a promise, able to see through His eternal foresight how it will all come to pass. God does not need to revise His plan as He goes, making adjustments and improvements as new information comes to light. No! He already knows it all and consequently makes the best promise the first time.

With such a God as this, we can put our full weight on Him, knowing without a doubt that He will do as He has said He will do. Since He is fully trustworthy, those of us who have trusted in Jesus Christ as Lord and Savior can look forward to one day joining Him in Heaven where Jesus is preparing a place for each of us. Seeing as God does what He says He will do, His children by faith can weather any storm knowing that He will use it all for our good, transforming us into the image of His Son. Because God is faithful and not wishy washy, it's only a matter of time before Jesus will come again to judge the living and the dead and to make all things right.

Even though God doesn't need to take an oath, since His own word is enough, He did so in order to set our minds at ease (Genesis 22:16). We can trust God at His Word because of who He is. Even though we are weak and feeble, prone to wander and doubt, He is strong and steady, never wavering in His guarantee, not ever questioning the wisdom of His decisions or wondering if there might be a better way. If God promised it, we can be confident it is the very best resolution possible and it's only a matter of time for it to come to pass. The only question, then, is whether or not we are going to wait patiently for God to deliver on His promises.

God said it, I believe it, That's good enough for me.
—Norman Hutchins

How do you doubt whether God has your best interest at heart?

_____

_____

When are you hesitating, holding back from putting your full weight on God and His promises?

_____

_____

Where do you think God might change His mind, suspecting He is just like the rest of us?

_____

_____

Heavenly Father,

You are a God who keeps His promises. You never go back on Your word nor are You surprised when circumstances change. Help me to trust You fully in Your sovereign power, so I can take You at Your Word. The Bible is filled with Your promises, and You are good for each of them. I admit that I sometimes don't believe what You say, doubting whether such goodness could be possible. I trust You fully this day to do as You have said You will do. I praise You for being the kind of God upon Whom I can rely. You are faithful, and my very life depends upon this faithfulness.

In Jesus' Name I pray. Amen

21
A Better Hope

"Now there have been many of those priests, since death prevented them from continuing in office; but because Jesus lives forever, he has a permanent priesthood. Therefore, he is able to save completely those who come to God through him, because he always lives to intercede for them.

Such a high priest truly meets our need—one who is holy, blameless, pure, set apart from sinners, exalted above the heavens. Unlike the other high priests, he does not need to offer sacrifices day after day, first for his own sins, and then for the sins of the people. He sacrificed for their sins once for all when he offered himself. For the law appoints as high priests men in all their weakness; but the oath, which came after the law, appointed the Son, who has been made perfect forever" (Hebrews 7:23-28).

She tries hard to do the right thing but often fails. Even when her actions appear good, her heart is off, her attitude wrong. There is this underlying feeling that she must do better, build something out of her life, make a significant difference; otherwise she feels useless and insignificant. Guilt and regret cloud her days and she can't seem to shake this feeling of foreboding.

This is the life we live when we try to walk according to the old covenant; the promise that was based on following the law and offering sacrifices when we failed to live up to His impossible standard of perfection. God's commandments and rules cannot save us from our sin, our tendency to live our own way instead of God's. Since God demands perfect obedience to the law, we are doomed to destruction when we live according to His rules. The only thing God's law is good for is showing us how hopelessly wrong we are.

Where is the hope in trying to live up to God's impossibly high standards, in attempting to please Him by how well we comply, in doing our best only to discover it is never good enough? No wonder we feel such guilt and shame, like we're complete failures: We can never work our way into God's good graces. As Mark Twain said, "If (Heaven) went by merit, you would stay out, and your dog would go in."

So where is our hope? Not in how well we perform, how dedicated we are to God's cause, or how faithful we are to a religious pursuit. The hope that we have here in the 21st century is a new hope; a confidence in a God who became man in order to offer Himself as the final, permanent sacrifice for all the ways we offend holy God. A promise that we can live forever as a part of God's loving family by faith in Jesus Christ, not because of bloodline or effort, but by the anticipation of God's presence throughout our lives, and not based on how well we live, but by how perfectly His Son obeyed.

Our place in the book of Life is secure, not based on merit or determination or even attitude, but purely grounded in what Jesus has done. Only Christ could deliver such a hope as this. And only Christ could do what the law could never do: save us from our sin. Through faith in Him, we have the security of belonging to the One who made us, the pleasure of living the abundant life He created us to live while looking forward to a joyful eternity with Him where we will be completely and wholly fulfilled and content. Doesn't this inspire more confidence than in trying hard and hoping in the end that we did enough? Yes, Jesus gives us the better hope.

An expectation for a better tomorrow
by the sweat of our brow,
Is a dim hope indeed.
A confidence that what is to come
is better than what is now here
by the sacrifice of Jesus, the perfect High Priest,
is the best hope of all!

How do you try to earn your way to Heaven by what you do?

_____

_____

In what areas of your life do you feel a sense of nagging guilt over how you continue to fail? Would it help to know that you are not judged by your ability to comply but by Jesus' permanent and powerful sacrifice?

_____

_____

Where are you failing to trust in what Jesus has already done for you?

_____

_____

Heavenly Father,

I admit that I often try to work my way to Heaven or impress You with my efforts and attitude. In reality, I know that Jesus is my only hope. Not only that, He is a greater hope than anything I can find in myself. Help me to honor the sacrifice You have made by putting my full weight on Jesus. I look forward to the peace that will come as I rest in what Jesus has already done, and let go of my attempts to earn your grace. I love You and want to live my life with You and through You.

In Jesus' Name I pray, Amen

22

A Better Priest

"Now the main point of what we are saying is this: We do have such a high priest, who sat down at the right hand of the throne of the Majesty in heaven, and who serves in the sanctuary, the true tabernacle set up by the Lord, not by a mere human being.

Every high priest is appointed to offer both gifts and sacrifices, and so it was necessary for this one also to have something to offer. If he were on earth, he would not be a priest, for there are already priests who offer the gifts prescribed by the law. They serve at a sanctuary that is a copy and shadow of what is in heaven. This is why Moses was warned when he was about to build the tabernacle: 'See to it that you make everything according to the pattern shown you on the mountain.' But in fact the ministry Jesus has received is as superior to theirs as the covenant of which he is mediator is superior to the old one, since the new covenant is established on better promises" (Hebrews 8:1-6).

It was never quite finished. We gave the dollhouse to my younger sister that Christmas long ago even though the shingles had not been glued onto the roof, the finishing details had not been completed and the cute little house had not even been furnished. Still, the deadline had come so we had to place it under the tree to be discovered on Christmas morning. Through the months to come we all worked on that dollhouse, but as cute as it was, it was never quite finished. It may have been a bigger project than anyone had imagined it would be; perhaps we bit off more than we could chew.

This incomplete dollhouse of my youth reminds me of God's kingdom. It's not finished. Things are not yet as they will be when God's perfect plan comes to fruition in His perfect time. Until then, though, when we will be united and live in harmony with Father, Son and Holy Spirit, Jesus sits in the position of power and honor at His Father's right hand.

In such a place, Jesus can perfectly intercede for us, pleading our case before the Righteous Judge, using His blood as a bargaining chip of sorts where His perfection becomes our own and the God of high standards is appeased. He also sacrificed Himself as the one-time offering that ended the curse of sin for all who would believe, taking away the sting of death and rendering helpless the power of sin and death in our lives through faith in Jesus Christ. At God's right hand, Jesus extends this authority to His sheep, giving us the power to persevere over sin, to overwhelm the enemy of our soul, and to live victoriously while we await our entrance into Heaven.

So, until all things are made right in the end, when Satan, the Prince of this dark world is flung into the lake of fire and there is no sin to keep us from relating to God as perfectly loved children, we have much hope. We have Jesus the Overcomer to give us confidence when it seems all is lost. Until this Enemy is placed under the feet of Jesus, we can be sure that his power in our lives is limited. When the lure of sin is strong, we have been given the authority to vanquish its domination and the power to withstand its attraction. Through the Superior Priest, we are never banished from the family of God as His blood protects us from God's righteous and rightful wrath.

God established the system of offerings and blood sacrifices to satisfy His need for justice in light of a fallen world where sin runs rampant. Through Jesus, this practice is made perfect, fully satiating God's appetite for an honest and fair verdict. While we were declared guilty, our Intercessor mediated a repealed death sentence that now means a new life for us through faith. While everything is not yet as it is meant to be, Jesus sits as our perfect High Priest at the right hand of God, making all the difference in the world and in our lives.

Jesus Christ turns life right-side-up,
and heaven outside-in.
—Carl F.H. Henry

How do you fail to utilize the power over sin Jesus delivers to you through His blood?

_____

_____

When are you living in despair instead of in the hope you have in Christ?

_____

_____

How do you feel hopeless in your situation, forgetting that Jesus interceded to deliver you the greatest hope of all?

_____

_____

Heavenly Father,

I admit I have no hope within myself yet I yearn for something to grab onto. Through Jesus, I have the confidence of knowing I'm accepted by You and will one day join You in the place that's been prepared for me. Help me to live victoriously until then, through faith in the perfect High Priest who sits at Your right hand. Thank You for making provisions for my sin, giving me Jesus who made Himself the permanent sacrifice for my sins so that I can live the life You meant me to live. I praise You for Your perfect plan and trust in Your timing to bring it into fulfillment as I live securely in Your good graces.
In Jesus' Name I pray, Amen

23

A Better Sanctuary

"Now the main point of what we are saying is this: We do have such a high priest, who sat down at the right hand of the throne of the Majesty in heaven, and who serves in the sanctuary, the true tabernacle set up by the Lord, not by a mere human being.

Every high priest is appointed to offer both gifts and sacrifices, and so it was necessary for this one also to have something to offer. If he were on earth, he would not be a priest, for there are already priests who offer the gifts prescribed by the law. They serve at a sanctuary that is a copy and shadow of what is in heaven. This is why Moses was warned when he was about to build the tabernacle: 'See to it that you make everything according to the pattern shown you on the mountain.' But in fact the ministry Jesus has received is as superior to theirs as the covenant of which he is mediator is superior to the old one, since the new covenant is established on better promises" (Hebrews 8:1-6).

The law said, "Do not kill." Jesus took it a step further and said anyone who has hate or ill-will in his heart against another is guilty of murder. Moses taught, "Do not commit adultery." Jesus upped the ante by saying that just looking at someone in lust is the same as physically breaking this mandate. The greatest commandment is to love the Lord with all your heart, soul and mind and the second is to love your neighbor as yourself. Jesus pushes us further by teaching the impossible, saying to "Love your enemies" (Matthew 5).

The law was only a shadow of what was to come. When Jesus came to earth as a man and died the death we were meant to die, He unveiled a new covenant based on grace, and received through faith, and set forth the true Temple, where we can all worship in Spirit and in Truth. This building is the model used by Moses to build the tabernacle so long ago in the desert. Not that it looks like the tent of meeting used by the people of Israel to offer sacrifices and tangibly feel God's presence, but it is the spiritual equivalent of the physical. In other words, the Old Testament temple was but a shadow of the church we have in Christ. He is the cornerstone of a spiritual building that is being constructed by God Himself, with the same meticulous attention to detail Moses took in building the tabernacle. Furthermore, this newly built tabernacle houses the Spirit of God, just as the one so long ago did.

This new temple, however, is not just a replacement for the old but is superior in many ways. It is made by God, not by man, and He uses us as His building blocks. Making it even more excellent is the fact that Christ himself is the corner-stone, resulting in a foundation that is secure and steady. As if this weren't enough, there is more: the Spirit dwells in us, freely accessed by a sinful people thanks to the redemptive blood of Jesus making us right by faith. Now, we can worship God in the way we live our lives and in how we relate to Him, not just in religious rituals and attention to the law, making this new temple even better. Our faith becomes a relationship and a lifestyle, not just an empty religion that is impotent to save us.

This sanctuary that is our heart, then, is the true Tabernacle where Christ is King and Priest, where God can be revealed in His true character, and where He has His way in every detail of our lives. In this, this new kind of church, which is composed of His people and headed by Christ Himself we truly see a superior Tabernacle: you and me.

Church is not a building or a place,
It is you and me living in relationship
with Christ and each other,
With Christ Himself as the Cornerstone.

How do you live as if your life is just a series of rules and duties instead of a passionate romance with the Lover of your soul?

_____

_____

When do you look at the church as a physical building instead of a spiritual place being constructed using real people by a God who loves us?

_____

_____

How can being a part of a church like this change the way you see God?

_____

_____

Heavenly Father,

I admit I live too much in the physical realm, failing to see how You are building me into this great Tabernacle where You are worshipped by those who love You. You are so much bigger and cannot be confined to a structure built by men. Instead, You have made a way to live in each of those who have given their lives to You, making us into a wonderful church where You are truly honored as Lord. Thank you for this superior Tabernacle which will never crumble or fade away. Help me to always revere You as Lord of my life.

In Jesus' Name I pray, Amen

24
Fully Revealed

"For if there had been nothing wrong with that first covenant, no place would have been sought for another. But God found fault with the people and said: 'The days are coming,' declares the Lord, 'when I will make a new covenant with the people of Israel and with the people of Judah. It will not be like the covenant I made with their ancestors when I took them by the hand to lead them out of Egypt, because they did not remain faithful to my covenant, and I turned away from them, declares the Lord. This is the covenant I will establish with the people of Israel after that time,' declares the Lord. 'I will put my laws in their minds and write them on their hearts. I will be their God, and they will be my people. No longer will they teach their neighbor, or say to one another, "Know the Lord," because they will all know me, from the least of them to the greatest. For I will forgive their wickedness and will remember their sins no more.'

By calling this covenant 'new,' he has made the first one obsolete; and what is obsolete and out-dated will soon disappear" (Hebrews 8:7-13).

It used to be a kind of mystery. Who was this God who led them out of slavery in Egypt, wrote the law on stone tablets with His own finger, and ushered them through the River Jordan on dry land, delivering the land promised to them? God's people knew

He was powerful, prone to anger and to be feared. But who was He, really? Could He be known as one knows His mother, brother, or lover? Is He a real person with feelings and desires, or just an aloof entity with no human-like qualities at all?

These questions that could have been asked by the Israelites are now answered in the Person of Jesus Christ. He came to establish a new covenant with His people, an agreement based on grace and delivered through faith. This mighty God who thundered over Mt Sinai is now readily available as a loving Shepard who tenderly tends His sheep. Not that He has changed in His character one iota, but that the one thing that separated us from Him, sin, which made it difficult for us to know Him, has been rendered powerless by the potent and permanent sacrifice of Jesus. When He shed His blood, He ushered in a new age where the Holy One of Israel is able to be known, is approachable and no longer obscured by a thick curtain.

Neither are His ways a mystery any longer. Each heart that is dedicated to Him is convicted by His law that is written on our hearts. When we're about to cross the line, remembrance of His better way of living comes to mind, causing a crisis of faith of sorts. Do I continue down this path which He clearly did not mean for me to follow, or turn around and head back toward Him? One ends in heartache, the other in peace and fulfillment.

The new covenant canceled out the old way of living where the law was supreme. We are no longer bound to following a set of rules, depending upon our compliance as a way to please God and earn His good grace. Now we are accepted freely as His children based on what Jesus did on the cross, giving us a new way of living as a wholly loved son or daughter where following Him replaces doing as the law commands. Staying close to Jesus and paying attention to His lead guarantees I will never do that which dishonors God or goes against His wishes. Our Shepherd will never lead us astray. This is the new covenant. This is the promise of grace through faith in Jesus Christ.

God's wisdom is not first counsel on how to practice
family values or to use common sense.
It is the wisdom of His plan of grace,
the wisdom of the Cross.
That wisdom is foolishness
to the calculations of prudence.
—Edmund P. Clowney

How do you live according to the old covenant, trying hard to follow the law, thus forsaking the person of Jesus Christ who wants so much to be known?

_____

_____

When do you put all your effort into knowing more about God, yet fail to invite Him into the deepest parts of your heart where you can know and be known?

_____

_____

Do you often fail to see God as a living Person, able to be known and with a great desire to be pursued by you?

_____

_____

Heavenly Father,

I admit I have de-personalized You, making You into this cold, standoffish Being who is too busy to bother with the likes of me. In reality, You want relationship with me, a deep, meaningful connection to me as Your child. Help me to let go of my desire to live according to a religion, the old covenant, and fully embrace the opportunity to get to know You through the new covenant delivered by Jesus Christ. Give me a heart for You so that I will want nothing more in life than to know You more.
In Jesus' Name I pray, Amen

25
Inwardly Clean

"The blood of goats and bulls and the ashes of a heifer sprinkled on those who are ceremonially unclean sanctify them so that they are outwardly clean. How much more, then, will the blood of Christ, who through the eternal Spirit offered himself unblemished to God, cleanse our consciences from acts that lead to death, so that we may serve the living God! For this reason Christ is the mediator of a new covenant, that those who are called may receive the promised eternal inheritance—now that he has died as a ransom to set them free from the sins committed under the first covenant" (Hebrews 9:13-15).

You remember the confrontation, don't you? It started off as a warning to the crowds following Jesus but quickly turned to criticism against the Jewish religious leaders. These were the men who everyone looked to for Biblical teaching, who set the standard, who gave them godly advice. They demanded esteem and honor. And here was Jesus, so-called Messiah, dragging them through the mud.

"Woe to you, teachers of the law and Pharisees, you hypocrites! You clean the outside of the cup and dish, but inside they are full of greed and self-indulgence. Blind Pharisee! First clean the inside of the cup and dish, and then the outside also will be clean" (Matthew 23:25-26). Is this the way to talk to these respected men of God?

Jesus could see behind the façade these men had carefully crafted and He was downright angry at how they were leading people astray, laying heavy burdens of guilt by creating their own yardstick to which even they themselves couldn't measure up, and lording their position and power over those they led. So, Jesus let them have it. He told them what He really thought of them and their pious, self-righteous ways. But what was truly the problem? Could there be more to living for God than just following a set of rules and being good at sticking to a religion that was meant to honor Him?

The law never saved anyone. Instead, the Word of God only showed the people when they had sinned, giving them reason to go to the altar to make sacrifices that would atone for their transgressions. But, as we can see with these corrupt leaders, the sacrifices did nothing for the heart. It did not institute real change. Instead, it only dealt with the outward manifestation of a sinful heart. The sacrifices of old had no effect on one's conscience or in renewing the inner man or of cleansing the heart (v 9).

But we are no longer under this old covenant of the law. It is no more about jumping through hoops, following instructions for proper worship and sacrifice, or observing the letter of the law. Instead, the High Priest who gave Himself as the final, perfect and spiritual sacrifice was able to touch the heart. Jesus' sacrifice reached where no other sacrifice was able to go. Jesus' death on the cross cleansed us from all unrighteousness and ushered in the age of the heart. Now it is the inside that is of more importance. Once we get our inner selves cleansed by Christ, the outward appearance will change accordingly. If, however, we get it backwards and try to change the outward appearance first, the heart will still be dirty, just like with the Pharisees, and we'll start to act like them too, pointing a judgmental finger toward others, expecting more from them than from ourselves, and seeing ourselves as better than we are. Through Christ we are made clean through and through, so we can live free of the burden of judgment and condemnation. Jesus liberates us!

Let us operate under the new covenant
where our great High Priest, Jesus Christ,
gives us a new heart, causing us not to just
appear clean, but to truly make us pure
from the inside out.

How are you focused on the outward appearance, completely ignoring the state of your heart?

_____

_____

When do you spend time looking at what others look like but forsake your own intentions and motives?

_____

_____

Have you let Jesus come into your life and make you white as snow?

_____

_____

Heavenly Father,

Thank You for Your grace and mercy in sending Jesus to make me white as snow. I confess I often try to appear to be better than I am, thinking I can fool others into thinking of me as spiritual or holy. In reality, my heart is dark, and I'm often driven by my own impulses and desires. I want You to be Lord of my life, leading me down paths of righteousness for Your namesake. Help me to surrender all to You, so that I can truly live the life Jesus died to give me. I love You!

In Jesus' Name I pray, Amen

26
Blood is Necessary

"In the case of a will, it is necessary to prove the death of the one who made it, because a will is in force only when somebody has died; it never takes effect while the one who made it is living. This is why even the first covenant was not put into effect without blood. When Moses had proclaimed every command of the law to all the people, he took the blood of calves, together with water, scarlet wool and branches of hyssop, and sprinkled the scroll and all the people. He said, 'This is the blood of the covenant, which God has commanded you to keep.' In the same way, he sprinkled with the blood both the tabernacle and everything used in its ceremonies. In fact, the law requires that nearly everything be cleansed with blood, and without the shedding of blood there is no forgiveness" (Hebrews 9:16-22).

"'I apologize to my classmates,' Asher concluded. He smoothed his rumpled tunic and sat down.

'We accept your apology, Asher.'"

What if life was like it was in the fictional, futuristic community depicted in Lois Lowry's 1993 novel, *The Giver*? Listening to the pleasant words expressed would make you think all was well, emotions were dealt with and pain and suffering were eliminated. In reality, this so-called "Sameness" was anything but deep and meaningful.

Instead, polite words were spoken but amounted to nothing more than an automatic pleasantry. The pardon offered in response to an apology didn't really mean anything.

What about forgiveness in our world, is it significant, or is it just an empty pleasantry; words spoken by an impotent god who wishes to give false hope to a gullible people? If God blindly issues clemency for falling short of His standard, would that forgiveness be worth anything?

God proves the worth of His forgiveness through the requirement of blood sacrifice. In order to sanctify an oath, making it worth trusting, God requires it to be backed-up with blood. The blood of Jesus made up for our sins, making it possible for forgiveness to be delivered to us by faith and lending weight to His offer of clemency. Without the shedding of blood, then, it's impossible to extend forgiveness because the debt stands unpaid. Without a blood sacrifice, mercy cannot be granted because the offense has not been addressed. Without an unblemished blood offering, the penalty merited for sin cannot be cancelled because the punishment due has not been assumed.

A judge who is worth his salt must mix mercy and justice, otherwise his rulings will be virtually meaningless. If he one day decides to offer forgiveness to a criminal, and the next day indiscriminately hands down a guilty verdict, he will soon be discredited for his bias. God, on the other hand, is a completely righteous Judge who requires punishment for every crime committed against Him. Out of His mercy, He accepts the blood of Jesus as atonement for my sin and yours, guaranteeing true forgiveness for all who believe.

It reminds me of a story told by Jeffrey Ebert. When he was five years old, he and his family were involved in a head-on collision with a drunk driver. During the era when riding in a car without a seatbelt was the norm, little Jeffrey sat on the lap of his mother in the front seat. When she saw the headlights coming toward them, she curled her body around his to protect him from the impact, taking the brunt of the crash herself. The force of the collision badly injured her body while Jeffrey walked away unscathed, yet covered by his mother's blood. She recovered after extensive surgery, but it left him with a lasting impression of the significance of Jesus' sacrifice for him. Without the blood of Jesus covering our sins, we have no hope of survival from the impact our sinful selves make when facing the righteousness and justness of God.

*Forgiveness offered apart from the shedding
of blood is no forgiveness at all.*

How do you think God can casually grant you forgiveness just because He's God, forgetting that the clemency comes with a price?

_____

_____

When do you allow sin into your life, forgetting the steep price Jesus paid to give you access to God's forgiveness?

_____

_____

How can you show greater appreciation for the sacrifice Jesus made for you?

_____

_____

Heavenly Father,

I don't often think of the price that was paid so that You can forgive me of my sins. I admit that I take Your forgiveness for granted, trusting that it'll always be there yet not realizing how expensive it is for You to freely give it to me. Help me to treasure this forgiveness as the costly gift that it is. May I live each day in the freedom Jesus' blood bought me, striving to abide in constant connection to You; not because I must, but because I can through the forgiveness bought for me by the blood of Jesus. I am forgiven.

In Jesus' Name I pray, Amen

27
Once is Enough

"It was necessary, then, for the copies of the heavenly things to be purified with these sacrifices, but the heavenly things themselves with better sacrifices than these. For Christ did not enter a sanctuary made with human hands that was only a copy of the true one; he entered heaven itself, not to appear for us in God's presence. Nor did he enter heaven to offer himself again and again, the way the high priest enters the Most Holy Place every year with blood that is not his own. Otherwise Christ would have had to suffer many times since the creation of the world. But he has appeared once for all at the culmination of the ages to do away with sin by the sacrifice of himself. Just as people are destined to die once, and after that face judgment, so Christ was sacrificed once to take away the sins of many; and He will appear a second time, not to bear sin, but to bring salvation to those who are waiting for Him" (Hebrews 9:23-28).

God has been drawing me to Jesus ever since I can remember. I recall attending vacation bible school with a friend at the age of five when I heard the gospel message and went forward to accept Jesus. When I came home, I prayed again as I sat on the edge of my bunk bed, feet dangling off the end. I still didn't feel anything so, not sure if it "took," I tried to remember the exact wording of the special prayer said in the church. *Did Jesus save me? Am I forgiven?* I wasn't sure.

It's common to lack the assurance of our salvation, especially when the acceptance is not accompanied by thunder from Heaven or some other dramatic experience. Satan wants nothing more than to keep us living in dread of our final destination, insecure as to our acceptance into God's kingdom, and wondering if we're truly forgiven so we'll live a life wracked with guilt and fear.

What if Jesus suffered from this same lack of faith? What if He did His part, giving His life on the cross as the final sacrifice for the sin of all mankind, yet He doubted whether or not it was enough? What if Christ thought it necessary to continue offering Himself on behalf of His sheep, dying over and over again to make sure He had done enough? As exaggerated and ridiculous as this seems, it's similar to what we do when we doubt our salvation.

Jesus bore our sin on the cross, taking the punishment meant for you and me. When He willingly let Himself be nailed to the cross, giving up His Spirit, He uttered the words, "It is finished." He was not just saying that His life was over, that His part was done. What Jesus was assuring us was that in His death, our sins had been atoned for and forgiveness had been granted. Jesus wanted us to know that restoration of the relationship man once enjoyed with his Creator had now been secured, as long as our faith is fully placed in Jesus Christ to lead us exclusively and rule over us supremely from that day forward."

The sacrifice of Jesus was the final blood offering perfectly made on behalf of everyone who believes, but it also ushered us into the age of the High Priest where Jesus sits at the right hand of the righteous Judge, pleading our case until He comes again. So you see, this once-for-all sacrifice gives us confidence that we only need believe on Jesus once, and that's enough to secure us in His kingdom forever.

Jesus did enough on the cross
to secure my place in His kingdom.
I did enough to accept my place in His Kingdom
when I received His gift of salvation
and vowed to follow Him alone.
Now I can live with Him
free from condemnation forever.
Once is enough.

How do I fear the judgment of God, worrying that simply accepting the forgiveness offered through Jesus can't be enough to cover me?

_____

_____

When do I live as one condemned, plagued with worry and doubt when, in reality, my place as a child of God is secure?

How do I feel like I don't belong, like I'm hopelessly flawed and unfit for God's kingdom?

Heavenly Father,

I believe that Jesus died a powerful death on the cross to release His blood that completely covers all of my sins for all of time. Because of this wondrous act of mercy and grace, I can live as Your well-loved child forever. Help me to fathom such love. Give me a heart that desires to accept the gift of salvation You have given through Christ, and may I never doubt my security in Your good graces again. In Jesus' name I pray, Amen

28
What is to Come

"Just as people are destined to die once, and after that face judgment, so Christ was sacrificed once to take away the sins of many; and he will appear a second time, not to bear sin, but to bring salvation to those who are waiting for him" (Hebrews 9:27-28).

We found the house in the new area that fit our needs and spoke to our hearts. We knew this was where we were meant to live. After flying back home to the other side of the country, we sent a check for the earnest money to the seller, confirming our contract to buy the house. The house was promised to us; it was as good as ours even though we had yet to take possession of it.

Jesus' death on the cross is similar to the earnest money in that it secured our salvation, giving us the promise of our protection against the judgment of God, but that deliverance will not be ours until Jesus comes the second time. For now, we have the promise of God that Christ's blood was enough to release us from the inevitability of death as punishment for how we have fallen short of His perfect standard.

This second coming, then, will be a glorious time for those of us in Christ when we will receive what we have long awaited: His kingdom fulfilled as it is in Heaven. It is this future salvation which Christ will deliver when He comes "in his Father's glory with his angels," that will bring redemption to its completion, bringing the promise full-circle as Jesus returns to reign in more than just our hearts (Matthew 16:27).

This hopeful expectation we have of Christ's return reminds me of a story I heard from Ray Bakke. He told of a Glasgow professor named MacDonald and a Scottish chaplain who were both imprisoned by the Germans during World War II. MacDonald was held with the Americans and the chaplain with the Brits, strictly separated by a high wire fence. The Americans secretly listened to news from the outside through a homemade radio and passed the headlines on to the British through MacDonald, confidentially delivering the updates in the ancient Gaelic language to the chaplain through the fence.

One day, news of the surrender of the German high command came over the airwaves and was passed jubilantly on to the prisoners. Every man's spirit was transformed as they realized their release was imminent. Men sang, shouted, waved to the guards, and laughed at the dogs. Three days later, the German guards finally heard the news of their defeat and fled in the night, leaving the gates unlocked. The next morning, the Americans and British were free to go but they had truly been freed three days earlier by the news that the war was over.

We, too, have received the news of our freedom, although that liberty will not fully be realized until

Christ comes again. Let us live joyfully with the expectation of what has been secured for us in Christ. We have the promise of rescue from the penalty of death and can live as one who has been freed from the power, presence, and pleasure of sin. Even though we live in the enemy camp, surrounded by death and sin, it is not where we belong. We have so much more to look forward to.

The best way to prepare for the coming of Christ
Is to never forget the presence of Christ.
—William Barclay

How do you dread Jesus' second coming, fearing judgment when He is coming to bring salvation to those who believe?

_____

_____

How can you live in joyful expectation of what is to come instead of focusing on what is in the here and now?

_____

_____

Have you focused your eyes on the finish line, or are you watching your feet as you negotiate your way around the potholes and rocky places?

_____

_____

Heavenly Father,

I believe in my heart that I am saved through faith in Christ Jesus, yet I often live as if I were still a prisoner, bound to the sin that seems to define my soul. Help me to live as one set free as I wait with hopeful expectation for what You will deliver in Christ: true salvation!
In Jesus' Name, Amen

29

Guilt is Gone

"The law is only a shadow of the good things that are coming—not the realities themselves. For this reason it can never, by the same sacrifices repeated endlessly year after year, make perfect those who draw near to worship. Otherwise, would they not have stopped being offered? For the worshipers would have been cleansed once for all, and would no longer have felt guilty for their sins. But those sacrifices are an annual reminder of sins. It is impossible for the blood of bulls and goats to take away sins" (Hebrews 10:1-4).

Guilt weighs heavy, bearing down upon her as she strives to live for Christ, taking one step forward and three disappointing steps back. Angry that she can't seem to slip free from the sin that hangs on like an unwelcomed parasite. She asks herself, "Why can't I get this right?" Shame hovers over her like a dark cloud, obscuring her vision of the cross, of what Jesus has already done for her. Who will free her from this body of death? She feels hopeless, as if her righteousness depends upon her.

Thankfully, the truth is ever before her through Jesus Christ our Lord. In Christ there is no longer any condemnation. The guilty verdict has been reversed. The sentence repealed. While easy words to say, to rattle off as one dictates a memorized poem or school assignment, they must penetrate the heart to make a difference. Jesus came to set us free from sin and death.

Back in the day of the first covenant, regular sacrifices were a constant reminder of one's sin. Israelites were painfully aware of their sin because each transgression required a blood offering. They must have fully felt their imperfection, wholly realizing how far they fell short, and probably carried a sense of guilt that they couldn't live up to God's standard.

Today, under the second, superior covenant, we have Jesus who made the perfect and final sacrifice for our sins, once for all. We are no longer constantly being reminded of our sin through the need for regular atoning offerings. Instead, Jesus did it all when He gave His life, the perfect ransom, the sacrifice that permanently removed our sins from us "as far as the east is from the west" (Psalm 103:12a). Now we can live freely, sure of our forgiveness and security in His love.

Since we are under the new system where we are made holy by the once-for-all-time sacrifice of Jesus, let us live as if we were righteous before God despite our sinful flesh. Let us see ourselves as God sees us; sanctified and blameless through the blood of His son. Let us walk in peace with God through faith in Jesus Christ. Guilt is a thing of the past, innocence is ours through Christ.

Instead of living as one condemned
Let us live as one set free.
When Jesus sets us free
We are free indeed!

How do you beat yourself up for how you mess up? Are
you trying to live perfectly, thus setting up an impossible
standard based on the first covenant?

_____

_____

Have you truly tasted the grace of God delivered through
faith in Jesus?

_____

_____

How can you fully surrender your desire to earn your keep
and completely rest on what Jesus has done for you?

_____

_____

Heavenly Father,
    I know I am a sinner saved by grace, but sometimes I
forget or fail to fully comprehend the "saved by grace"
part. Help me to see how far You have removed my sin

from me so that I can live in the new covenant, free of guilt. Jesus died so that I wouldn't always have to have my sin before me, but sometimes I feel I deserve to suffer for how far I fall short. I don't feel worthy to live the abundant life Jesus died to give me. Today I place that faulty line of thinking on the Cross and accept as enough the suffering Jesus experienced on my behalf as enough. I want to fully rest on the Gospel of Jesus Christ, not on the teaching of the law that requires perfect adherence. Thank You for giving Your Son so that I might live by grace, rid of guilt once and for all.

In Jesus' Name I pray, Amen

30

Fit Like a Glove

"Therefore, when Christ came into the world, he said: 'Sacrifice and offering you did not desire, but a body you prepared for me; with burnt offerings and sin offerings you were not pleased. Then I said, "Here I am—it is written about me in the scroll—I have come to do your will, my God"'" **(Hebrews 10:5-7).**

"O Lord, grant that I may do thy will as if it were my will; so that thou mayest do my will as if it were thy will." Augustine penned these words centuries ago, yet they resonate strongly in today's world of self-will and identity. We want what we want, when we want it, delivered in the way we want it and in a way that is peculiar to us. In short, we are our own gods who are obsessed with ourselves.

What the ancient philosopher seemed to understand that is often missed in today's self-centered world is the heart of God. It is not so much what we do or how we appear that matters to Him, but the incline of our heart and the motives that drive our actions. It is His desire that we be so closely identified with Him that we can't tell where our own self ends and His begins, so that our desires cease being distinct from His own and our heart hurts for what breaks His. In other words, we must lose ourselves in Him.

Jesus didn't come to impress anyone with His fervor and dedication. He didn't find it necessary to win people over to His side. We never read about Him running after anyone who rejects Him, instead letting each make up their own mind. Christ didn't jump through hoops to meet people's needs, going out of His way to make them happy. He was not in a popularity contest. Rather, He acted when His heart was moved, putting feet to the compassion of His Father that flowed through his veins. He came to do His Father's bidding and it was only His Father's opinion that mattered to Him.

We can identify with Christ in this way. Even though we may feel pressure to conform, we are not here to please people, to win them over, to make others happy or to gain a following. Instead, we are here to obey the will of our Father. Our purpose is to simply enjoy intimacy with Him and to conform our will to His, drawing closer in relationship with Him each day.

I've heard it said that this kind of intimate relationship is similar to the comparison of a glove to the hand. The glove in and of itself has no power to move or perform any functions of a hand. For that, it needs a hand to slip in, filling every space inside. When it does, the fabric comes to life as the hand moves in the way only a hand can move. This gives the appearance that the glove is the one doing the work when really, it's the hand inside that deserves all the credit.

Thus it is with us and God. We are ourselves a useless shell in our own right, unable to do any of the work God can do. When we accept Jesus as Savior and His Spirit enters into our being, the more space we make for Him to fill, the more of His distinctness we detect. We see fruit; love, joy, peace, patience, kindness, goodness, faithfulness, gentleness, and self-control. While it may look like it is the person doing these amazing feats, it's really God who is the one working through the believer, in the same way the hand works through the glove.

Our job, then, is to make way for the Spirit of God in our lives, cooperating with His transforming work and surrendering in obedience to His will. In these ways we'll fit like a glove onto God, standing in amazement to see His mighty Hand at work.

We can't impress God
No matter how hard we try.
He is pleased, however,
When we make room for Him,
getting rid of more flesh each day,
making more space for Him to shine through.

How do you work hard at trying to look like a Christian, wasting precious time that could be spent honing your relationship with Christ?

_____

_____

Do you try to become Christ-like instead of letting Him have His way in your life, leading to this coveted outcome?

_____

_____

When do you ignore God's wishes and simply focus on what you think He would like?

_____

_____

Heavenly Father,

I see that I am made for You, to live in close relationship with You as I live my life. So often, though, I get that mixed up and think I am to live for me, in a way that impresses You and people. Help me to grow in my bond with You so that Your will becomes mine, and mine yours. May I strive to obey Your still, small voice and the convictions You place in my heart. Help me to break the habit of people pleasing and image promotion and simply live as Your well-loved child.
In Jesus' Name I pray, Amen

31
Made Holy

"First he said, 'Sacrifices and offerings, burnt offerings and sin offerings you did not desire, nor were you pleased with them'—though they were offered in accordance with the law. Then he said, 'Here I am, I have come to do your will.' He sets aside the first to establish the second. And by that will, we have been made holy through the sacrifice of the body of Jesus Christ once for all" (Hebrews 10:8-10).

Every item used in sacrifice had to be cleansed before use. There were specific requirements of what could be considered worthy of sacrifice; any old offering would not do. Even the priests who offered the sacrifices had to be of a certain bloodline and go through special rituals in order to sanctify themselves for the job. Under the old covenant, sacrifices and offerings made in the wrong way profaned God's holy name.

Jesus negates this covenant by His sacrifice on the cross. In the giving of Himself in order to appease God's perfect sense of justice, He made a way for God to set aside for His own use those who come to Him by faith in Christ. Through Jesus; the common became holy, the unclean became pure, and the profane became sacred.

Jesus made possible what animal sacrifice never could do: permanently cleanse us from sin. It used to be that it was the sacrifices that called for holiness. Now it is the one perfect Sacrifice that makes holiness possible for all who believe. No longer are we at risk of being labeled as unworthy. We can stop worrying that the very existence of our sinful flesh will offend God. There is no longer a concern that an unconfessed sin will condemn us to damnation. In Christ, we have been made holy by His one-time sacrifice.

But there's more. Under the old covenant, there was really no hope for the future, no regeneration of the heart, no transformation process. It merely consisted of living from sacrifice to sacrifice, letting each temporary fix atone for that month's sins without an expectation for a better tomorrow. It was up to one's effort and will to improve their compliance to the law.

Through Jesus, observance of the law has been proved to be useful merely as a humbling tool, showing us how far we fall short from God's perfect standard. Once we enter into a relationship with Jesus, by repenting of our sins and trusting Him as Lord and Savior, He begins the transformation process and each believer sees progress as we cooperate with His supernatural work within.

If we forget we have already been deemed as set apart for God and try to earn that position through effort, we soon run out of steam and get frustrated at our inability to improve behavior. Before we know it, we feel like we are spinning our wheels, unable to move forward in our journey of faith. A.W. Tozer put it this way, saying, "Think about people who find themselves in religious ruts. They discover a number of things about themselves. They will find that they are getting older but not getting any holier. Time is their enemy, not their friend. They were not any better last year than they had been the year before."

It is only the blood of Jesus that dedicates us for God's use, and only He that purifies us from all unrighteousness. As we live in submission to His work in our hearts, we find a sensitivity to the sin that is in us. As Oswald Chambers wrote, "The love of God working in me causes me to hate, with the Holy Spirit's hatred for sin, anything that is not in keeping with God's holiness." The work of His Spirit in us, then, produces holiness on a level we could never achieve on our own.

The old way used holy things to attempt righteousness. The new way used the Righteous One to bring about holiness in the unrighteous.

How do you attempt to prove your worth; working hard to try to be better, attempting to conquer sin, striving *for holiness?*

_____

_____

Have you sensed the regeneration of your heart, bringing spiritual transformation through Christ Jesus?

_____

_____

How do you feel guilty for all the ways you fall short, thinking you must try harder to reach perfection?

_____

_____

Heavenly Father,

I am becoming more and more aware of how impossible it is to live up to Your standard and how much I need Jesus. I believe that He came to set me free from this necessity, instead making me holy by faith. Help me to trust You to continue this transforming work, putting myself into Your capable hands. Give me courage to let go of my desire to control my own regeneration process and instead allow You full access to my heart and mind. Give me peace as I learn to love You fully, as You love me.
In Jesus' Name I pray, Amen

32
Perfect the Imperfect

"Day after day every priest stands and performs his religious duties; again and again he offers the same sacrifices, which can never take away sins. But when this priest had offered for all time one sacrifice for sins, he sat down at the right hand of God, and since that time he waits for his enemies to be made his footstool. For by one sacrifice he has made perfect forever those who are being made holy" (Hebrews 10:11-14).

It's hard for me to rest when there are jobs left undone. If there are dirty dishes in the sink, clutter covering the kitchen table, or repair projects lying half-finished, it's just difficult for me to kick my feet up and watch a movie or enjoy a game of Scrabble with my husband. I'd like to tie up all the loose ends before I can truly relax.

I wonder if Jesus is like this. I say this because Jesus sat down at the right hand of God after He had made the once-for-all sacrifice of His own perfect, sinless body on a cruel Roman cross. It's as if He rested in His proper place with a sigh, thinking "there, my work is done and now I can rest." After all, He had accomplished what all the years of sacrifices had never been able to bring about. No matter how many times the priests performed their religious duties, sin still remained and its power over the people kept them in guilt and unforgiveness, sending them back to the altar again and again. But Jesus, in His sacrifice, conquered sin and death, doing all that needed to be done for us who believe in Him. Through His shed blood, we are promised something that was never before possible: perfection.

Now this is not to say that those of us who are in Christ Jesus are without sin and will never again follow our fleshly desires. What is meant is that there is this promise of completion, that through the blood of Jesus we have entered into a purifying process which will one day end at the goal of complete purity. What Jesus has done does not present to us the end product (perfection) all tied up in a neat little bow, but a way for us to get to the completion of the sanctification process. It is the means to this end of wholeness and completeness which will one day be ours in eternity.

Jesus can rest because His work on the cross made it possible for us to enter into sanctification. Yes, we are new creatures in Christ, but the transformation is not yet complete. It will never be done in this life. But, in Christ we have every reason to look forward to the future because of what He has secured for us. That is why He sat down; because the job was finished. Now it is up to us to believe that completeness and perfection will one day be ours, and cooperate with the transformation process of the Holy Spirit that will get us to that point.

In Christ,
The new heart is ours
but sinlessness is only promised.

Our job?
To believe purity has been secured for us
by His well-finished work on the cross,
and press on toward the finish line.

How do you get discouraged because you keep failing? Do you unrealistically expect perfection now?

_____

_____

How do you feel like a failure, incapable of doing right? Would it help to know that Jesus is the One who did all that was necessary to give you what is impossible for you to attain yourself?

_____

_____

When are you striving for perfection instead of cooperating with the perfecting process of the Holy Spirit within you?

_____

_____

Heavenly Father,

I know how desperately sinful I am and incapable of pleasing You with my compliance to Your standard. Seeing that Jesus has already secured my entrance into the perfecting process that will not be finished in this life is a relief. Jesus is at rest because the hard work is already done, now it is my job to let You bring it to fruition. Help me to let go of my desire to make myself worthier, and simply let You do what Jesus secured for me. I want to be like moldable clay in Your hands.
In Jesus' name I pray, Amen

33

Forgiveness Secured

"For by one sacrifice he has made perfect forever those who are being made holy. The Holy Spirit testifies to us about this. First he says: 'This is the covenant I will make with them after that time, says the Lord. I will put my laws in their hearts, and I will write them on their minds.' Then he adds: 'Their sins and lawless acts I will remember no more.' And where these have been forgiven, sacrifice for sin is no longer necessary" (Hebrews 10:14-18).

The best efforts from the brightest minds gathered across time and culture could not come up with it. The most theologically astute scholars could never comprehend it. Even the most gracious and giving from among us could not mimic it. Only God could deliver this new and improved promise to all people who trust in Jesus as Lord and Savior.

What is it that He's done that was otherwise impossible? He supernaturally made a way for you and me to be led internally, to know what is the right way to go, to have a sense of what will please Him. It is not just the written Word that convicts, but the heart. It is now possible to undergo a transformation process as we spiritually follow our Savior down the path He has marked out for us. Instead of trying and failing to do what is right, we now can walk with the One who will never lead us wrong. We are internally led as opposed to trying to be externally compliant. We now have an inner Guide who leads us on paths of righteousness for His namesake.

Even more, we have forgiveness. In the past, the people of God did have a form of forgiveness, but it was partial and temporary, only lasting until the next sin was committed and the people were again found to be impure and needing of cleansing by the blood of the sacrifice. As they presented their offering to the priest who sacrificed it on their behalf to secure this temporary forgiveness, the transgressions committed were atoned for by the blood of the lamb. Once Jesus came and offered His own life, however, our sins were permanently covered by His blood, making us right with God by the blood of the Lamb, once and for all, completely and enduringly.

The wonder of this mercy and compassion offered by the One we have offended by our sin is astounding. Could it be that we will never stand guilty before the Judge of the living and the dead? Is it true that our sins are removed as far away from us as the east is from the west? While we're sinful to the core, do we appear to God as if we were pure as freshly fallen snow? Yes, by faith in Jesus Christ, it is true. Our forgiveness is secured. Let us never take that for granted.

The wonder of forgiveness has become a banality.
It can be the death of our faith if we forget that is literally
a miracle.
—Helmut Thielicke

How do you live as if you must earn the forgiveness Jesus died to give you?

_____

_____

When are you so afraid to disappoint God that you stay in your little corner, ceasing to venture out into the world?

_____

_____

Do you realize the forgiveness you have in Christ is whole and permanent?

_____

_____

Heavenly Father,

I know I am a sinner saved by grace through faith in Jesus Christ. Sometimes, however, I admit to trying to be a better person in my own strength, or I'm led by guilt to do things for You, or I live in fear of Your judgment. Help me to dwell in the peace that comes from being made right with You. Give me the assurance of Your forgiveness secured by Jesus. It is my desire to live freely the abundant life Jesus died to give me.
In Jesus' Name I pray, Amen

34
Take Advantage

"Therefore, brothers and sisters, since we have confidence to enter the Most Holy Place by the blood of Jesus, by a new and living way opened for us through the curtain, that is, his body, and since we have a great priest over the house of God, let us draw near to God with a sincere heart and with the full assurance that faith brings, having our hearts sprinkled to cleanse us from a guilty conscience and having our bodies washed with pure water" (Hebrews 10:19-22).

"I'd like you to be able to take advantage of this great deal only offered in the month of January." My dad was wanting to move into an assisted living facility where he could enjoy his own space yet still have the benefits of a caring staff, delicious meals and stimulating interaction with others. It sounded ideal, but it came with an expensive price tag. If we signed up now, however, we'd save thousands of dollars.

Salesman are good at setting up a need for what they're selling, then offering a deal we can't refuse. With such a bargain as this, who could say no? Jesus is no salesman pitching the latest product that we can't live without, but there is something He is offering of which we must take advantage. In His offer, however, He is the one who paid the steep price to gain us clear access to God, so what are we waiting for?

Well, for one thing, we often feel unworthy to be in His presence, to enter into such a holy place as this. *Who am I to petition God; to share my heart with Him, to express such deep thoughts to a God who is so much higher?* I am sinful to the core, unable to stand in His presence, right?

Yes, but the beauty of the Gospel is that Jesus parted the curtain that hung between a holy God and the people He loves, serving as the Great High Priest who delivered permanent atonement through His sacrifice so that we are made righteous. And when we do as Paul urges us to do, and "draw near to God with a sincere heart" and the confidence of our faith, we find a miraculous thing: He purifies us from the guilty conscience that often plagues us, the heavy weight of shame and sense of responsibility to bear our own sin.

Jesus made a way for us to enter into this sanctuary where we will find peace and fulfillment. We must take advantage of what Jesus is offering and come forward, treading on the hallowed ground of a holy God who is miraculously being extended as our approachable Father. If we are not treating Him as such, are we not making light of Jesus' sacrifice?

For all the times we stay away, choosing instead to follow a form of godliness, looking good to those who are watching but resisting the transforming work of the Holy Spirit within, are we not snubbing our noses at the horror Jesus faced on our behalf? Or what about when we come to God but dare not get too close lest He see our insincerity, the barrier we so carefully craft to keep others from seeing the ugly truth? Are we not refusing the redemption that comes through faith in Jesus Christ? Or when we doubt our atonement, that we could truly be forgiven, wondering if we are really saved or if there is a need to add to what has already been done? Does this not diminish the power of the saving blood of Jesus?

Jesus gave His all, suffering greatly to deliver the way to His Father. Will we not take advantage of such treasure? Let us not waste another minute!

It's done, the way made clear
What are you waiting for?
Come freely and eagerly to the One who loves you best.

When do you fail to take God up on His offer to come freely to Him?

_____

_____

How does your guilt keep you away from God, robbing you of the abundance He is offering through Christ?

_____

_____

Where can you let go of your tendency to try to work your way to God instead of taking the clear path?

_____

_____

Heavenly Father,

I am so grateful for the gift of salvation offered through Christ, but I confess I don't always take advantage of the guilt-cleansing I can experience in Your intimate presence. I keep my distance, afraid of Your judgment or misunderstanding the offer of freedom I have in You. Help me to boldly come as a well-loved child who can never lose her place in Your graces. Give me the courage to live the life Jesus died to give me.

In Jesus' Name I pray, Amen

35
How to Persevere

"Let us hold unswervingly to the hope we profess, for he who promised is faithful. And let us consider how we may spur one another on toward love and good deeds, not giving up meeting together, as some are in the habit of doing, but encouraging one another—and all the more as you see the Day approaching" (Hebrews 10:23-25).

The aisle is filled with self-help books, tomes overflowing with advice for living, step-by-step instructions on everything from how to go through the grieving process to how to make friends and influence people. There are even bestsellers that give us the secret to living a stress free life or the habits of the movers and shakers of this world.

Today's scripture passage is a how-to of sorts; a guide in how to persevere in this difficult life as we live in a broken world full of heartaches, pain and suffering. How do we keep going under such dire conditions, when loved ones die, marriages end, and children rebel? When friends betray, jobs are lost, and hopelessness prevails?

For one, we can't just speak what we believe and leave it at that. This faith which gives us every reason to have confidence in the future is meant to be taken to heart, to penetrate the very marrow of our bones so that when the unthinkable happens, the hope does not disappear. Instead, the courage that comes from our faith in Christ acts as an anchor that keeps us from being tossed around by the waves of life.

It reminds me of a recent windstorm that lasted for several days and included gusts of up to 80 mph. The first morning, one of the large doors on our barn suddenly pulled loose and began flapping like a flag in the wind. As we helplessly watched in horror, it ripped off, landing on the ground with a crash. If the door had been properly bolted closed, it would have been secure no matter how strong the wind.

This is like our faith. Our belief that God is faithful to be all He says He is gives us something to look forward to, reason to stand firm, an expectation for good to come out of the bad. It's like those bolts driven through the barn door: faith keeps us steady.

But what happens when we don't always feel it, like we're losing grasp of the Solid Rock? That is where our brothers and sisters in Christ come in, bolstering our faith with their words of truth, spurring us on to keep fighting the good fight, to continue loving and living with Jesus despite the hardness of such a thing. Our connection to the Body of Christ must be preserved and is vital to our well-being and ability to keep going.

We need look no further than the wisdom of God's Word to find instruction for how to continue on in the face of hardship or just in ordinary living. Jesus Christ gives us the hope to which we can cling, and we need each other as believers to remind us of these truths. As I've heard it said, "People are like stained-glass windows: they sparkle and shine when the sun is out. But in the darkness, beauty is seen only if there is a light within." Let Jesus be that Light inside!

God is faithful, this we know
And His Son gives strength to all who hope.
While fear and doubt toss us to and fro,
Faith in God grants the tools to cope.

How do you let the winds of life blow you wherever they may take you?

_____

_____

When do you need a dose of hope that Jesus Christ can deliver?

_____

_____

How are you doubting in God's ability to save you?

_____

_____

Heavenly Father,
I am weaker in faith than I'd like to admit. I need more of Jesus to make up for my shortcomings and desire that

He be my Rock which gives me firm footing in the storm. It is my prayer that I can keep my eyes on Him when the going gets rough and remember to lean on the family You have surrounded me with, so I can draw encouragement and inspiration from them. Help me to live with abandon; totally surrendered to You.

In Jesus' Name I pray, Amen

36
A Terrible Thing

"If we deliberately keep on sinning after we have received the knowledge of the truth, no sacrifice for sins is left, but only a fearful expectation of judgment and of raging fire that will consume the enemies of God. Anyone who rejected the law of Moses died without mercy on the testimony of two or three witnesses. How much more severely do you think someone deserves to be punished who has trampled the Son of God underfoot, who has treated as an unholy thing the blood of the covenant that sanctified them, and who has insulted the Spirit of grace. For we know him who said, 'It is mine to avenge; I will repay,' and again, 'The Lord will judge his people.' It is a dreadful thing to fall into the hands of the living God" (Hebrews 10:26-31).

He did the unthinkable, putting Himself in the hands of cruel and merciless men, even though He was meant to be revered and honored. Why did He succumb to beatings, taunting, scourging, torment, and a torturous death; especially from those who esteemed Him not, for those who thumbed their noses at Him, for those who didn't even bother to consider Him at all?

Jesus made the ultimate sacrifice for His own enemies, the very ones who defiled His creation with ugly and devastating sin. Who are these loathsome creatures? You and me; all of mankind to be exact. Everyone made in His image is fallen and broken, in need of saving from God's holy and righteous condemnation. So, Jesus came not to further doom us, but to save us from the sin that ruins us.

With such a mission as this, must we not step out of ourselves and see the big picture? It's easy to accept the sacrifice Jesus has made as what my friend calls "fire insurance" —protection against the eternal damnation our sin earns us. It's a very limited and self-serving perspective. But Jesus came for more than this, for more than just everlasting life, which is a pretty amazing benefit in itself. The package deal is greater than only what is to come when this life is over. He also came to sanctify us, to set us apart for His purposes, to conform us into His own image, to give us the opportunity to offer that which ordains us to be used for the sacred. This is all ours now.

Rejecting some of the offer while accepting the part we like makes a mockery of what Jesus has done. It is not true acceptance at all. Thinking we can take the ticket into Heaven, while refusing the hallowing of our lives, the holy plan He has for us, the sometimes-painful transformation process, the chance to be used as an instrument of righteousness is like trampling on Jesus; treating His precious blood which sealed the holy covenant as if it were common and profane, insulting the Spirit of God with scorn.

We are in jeopardy of fooling ourselves that we're exempt from the wrath of God if we prayed for salvation yet continue to act as if we're still unsaved. In fact, I would go a step further and do as Paul said in 2 Corinthians 1:3-5 and say, "Examine yourselves to see whether you are in the faith." If we willfully sin, knowing what we do is wrong, but figuring the blood of Jesus will save us, we are not thinking as one who is under His saving grace. Instead, we have scorned it.

Without the option of the first covenant's animal sacrifices, then, there is nowhere to turn for forgiveness apart from the offer from Christ. If we have turned down salvation through faith in Christ with our willfully sinful way of life, rejecting it in all intents and purposes, it no longer exists for us. Instead of living in such a way, let us turn away from the sin Jesus died to save us from and allow His transforming Spirit to change the way we think. Let Him give us a new reason for living and a new purpose for our bodies. Let us fully turn away from sin and toward Jesus, accepting all that He has for us and avoid the wrath of God. It is a terrible thing to fall into His hands without the protection of the blood that saves.

Jesus came to save, offering us His rescue.
With such a high price paid, I must never forget,
Stepping back into the lifestyle He came to destroy.
He came for more than this,
and it is my privilege to honor Him always.

Have I truly accepted the saving grace of God that comes through faith in Jesus Christ, or am I still testing the waters?

_____

_____

How do I show a failure to commit to Jesus, wanting the fire insurance without having to let go of my own fleshly desires?

_____

_____

Have I considered that my low view of sin, my failure to repent, is making a mockery of Jesus' death?

_____

_____

Heavenly Father,

It is hard for me to think of You as a dangerous God, but Your wrath is real, and I am not exempt from it apart from Jesus. He stands between, offering reconciliation, but rejecting His complete covenant will put me on the outside. I am under His protection unless I remove myself, suddenly wanting to live my old life without regard for what Jesus did for me. I know I am secure in Your love and You will never abandon me, and I would never want to dishonor such love by living as if it didn't exist. Your love transforms me into who You meant me to be, and I never want to go back to who I once was. Thank You for such a gift as this.

In Jesus' Name I pray, Amen

37
Firmly Press On

"Remember those earlier days after you had received the light, when you endured in a great conflict full of suffering. Sometimes you were publicly exposed to insult and persecution; at other times you stood side by side with those who were so treated. You suffered along with those in prison and joyfully accepted the confiscation of your property, because you knew that you yourselves had better and lasting possessions. So do not throw away your confidence; it will be richly rewarded.

You need to persevere so that when you have done the will of God, you will receive what he has promised. For, 'In just a little while, he who is coming will come and will not delay.' And, 'But my righteous one will live by faith. And I take no pleasure in the one who shrinks back'" (Hebrews 10:32-38).

No one likes to be on the outside looking in, to feel like the odd-man out. As humans, we crave feeling like we belong, as if we are a part of a group, making it hard to stand out with a differing opinion or belief.

This reminds me of a story I once heard from a well-known psychologist who attended a mandatory staff introductory course at the hospital where he recently began working. All the new employees were required to attend, no matter their position or background. As they started the meeting, the leader asked the multi-generational group if they'd like some refreshments. Not wanting to be the only one to rise from their chair and approach the table laden with drinks and snacks, every person declined her offer. Finally, the older professional could see what was happening and decided to break the ice. Once he grabbed a drink and something to eat, almost everyone in the room followed suit. It's not that no one was hungry or thirsty. Rather, no one wanted to go against the group-think or the majority opinion.

This human trait is important to realize as we live in a world that is bound to present ideas that are in opposition to what the Gospel proclaims. It's easy to keep quiet when a word of loving yet unpopular insight could bring enlightenment. When everyone else is agreeing with what you know in your heart is not the truth, it takes courage to speak out, going against the crowd. When it seems the whole group is enthusiastically defending what is not God's best for us, it takes confidence in one's beliefs to stand out from the mainstream.

Likewise, it takes a strong belief in the Gospel to stand firm in the face of persecution. If we are ridiculed, or even simply questioned, we will not be able to stand up against it unless we believe it to be true. We live by faith when we rejoice in our sufferings, knowing it brings with it a certain commonness with Christ himself. He was ridiculed for being called the King of the Jews. He was scourged for claiming divinity. He was killed for ruffling the feathers of the powers that be. As His followers, we can expect some of the same treatment.

How can we stand up against the majority and refrain from shrinking back when the going gets tough? How will we, in the face of persecution, be able to draw from the Spirit of power, love and a sound mind that God gives us? We can reject our natural tendency to shrink back, to hesitate, to withdraw our voice by remembering what we do now impacts eternity. If we persevere, we receive the crown rewarded to those who prove their genuine dedication to God and Christ, who cross the finish line with the intent to win the prize. So we press on, not needing to have all the answers but simply knowing the One who does, and being confident in our faith in Him, trusting that He will give us all the words we need to proclaim the reason for the hope that we have.

> *To cling to God and to the things of God —*
> *This must be our major effort,*
> *This must be the road that the heart follows.*
> —John Cassian

How do you back down under the face of opposition?

_____

_____

When are you afraid to stand out from the crowd, even if the majority is spreading a message that leads to destruction?

_____

_____

How can thinking of your reward for persevering give you the motivation to keep running your race with conviction?

_____

_____

Heavenly Father,

I am easily deterred from the mission at hand, forgetting of my heavenly home and living instead for the here and now. Help me to keep my eyes on where my hope lies, standing strong for what I know to be true and keeping the faith when I feel like giving up. I know You are faithful to give me the strength that I need, and I want to trust You to do so, even in the face of great persecution. Give me an eternal focus that motivates me to run the best race I can run, for Your glory.
In Jesus' Name I Pray, Amen

38
Faith, or Faith in God?

"Now faith is confidence in what we hope for and assurance about what we do not see. This is what the ancients were commended for. By faith we understand that the universe was formed at God's command, so that what is seen was not made out of what was visible" (Hebrews 11:1-3).

Voltaire, 18th century writer, historian and philosopher, thought that, "Faith consists in believeing when it is beyond the power of reason to believe." There is something in us that is drawn to faith, that wants to believe everything will turn out okay, and that longs to have confidence in the midst of the blackest unknown. We strive to keep a positive attitude in life, hoping our thoughts will manifest themselves in reality; that what we believe will happen will actually happen. This is the essence of faith; it is marching forward with the conviction that what we envision will come to pass.

There is some mystery interwoven into faith. If we could see all the steps laid out in front of us or understand the reasoning behind the path chosen for us or were able to perceive how it will all end, living wouldn't take faith at all. If we had all the answers, possessed perfect foresight, and enjoyed complete comprehension of all things, we would be like God and wouldn't need faith.

The truth is, we don't know it all, see it all, or get it all. We need the power to trust that our hope is not blind or in vain, but will amount to something positive, to bring about what we are waiting for. But all this talk about faith doesn't mean a thing without a focal point toward which to direct the faith. Just to hope, without a power to hope in, seems like blind hope to me. In other words, it seems more like wishful thinking if I have no object for my faith.

For instance, I can believe that the world came about slowly, over time, beginning with a few basic building blocks; that everything that is known and can be seen by man was made out of what could not be seen. I guess that could fall under the heading of the Big Bang Theory or Evolution. It takes faith to believe such a thing, does it not? To consider that life came from the muck, that all the millions of life forms came from just one. Yes, this takes faith.

But there is always a question left unanswered in this kind of undirected faith; namely, by what power did this all come about? From where did the energy come to generate such an explosion as to set the solar system into place? How did such order come from chaos? Can I really chalk it all up to happenstance?

What I'm trying to get at is that in order to have faith, we must have faith in *something*. We can believe our friends will come through and throw a wonderful birthday party, or we can just hope it will somehow happen. One is trusting in the integrity and knowledge of people I know who are capable of creating such an event, the other simply places that faith in nothing specific, but just casts it out into nothingness.

For faith to be real, it must be placed in something or someone. Faith must have an object. When we place our faith in God, He will not let us down, which is for what the Hall of Faithers were commended. These people of old trusted that God would come through, that He would make good on His word, that He would follow His pattern started at the beginning and make something out of nothing.

We can do the same today. We can trust God to take the shambles of our broken lives and create a masterpiece of beauty and order, or we can just believe it will happen. We can have faith in God to soften a hardened heart, mend a broken relationship, or give sight to the blind, or we can just believe it will happen. We can accept that God is able to give us the abundant life Jesus came to deliver, to exchange mourning for joy, to transform despair into praise, or we can just believe it will happen.

For a faith to grow in us that is worthy of the Faith Hall of Fame, we must place our faith in God. Now this is the kind of faith on which we can stake our lives!

Faith is no faith at all if it is not placed in
the One who is worthy of such belief.

How do you blindly believe good will come without knowing from whom all good things come?

_____

_____

When do you hope for the best without knowing the One who has your best in the palm of His hand?

_____

_____

Heavenly Father,

I rejoice that You are in control of all things and that Your power is worthy of my faith. I often want to believe the best in people or of my life, but I see that only You can carry such a responsibility. I want to place all my faith in You who can make it all come about. Nothing is impossible with You, and I do not want to trust in any other power than You alone. May my faith continue to grow as I believe all things come from You. You are the faithful One who can handle the expectations I have for You to accomplish. You will never let me down.

In Jesus' Name I pray, Amen

39

Set His Heart to Singing

"By faith Abel brought God a better offering than Cain did. By faith he was commended as righteous, when God spoke well of his offerings. And by faith Abel still speaks, even though he is dead" (Hebrews 11:4).

Busy, busy, busy. This could describe the normal modern life. And if we follow Jesus, we take that same mindset into His kingdom, applying the adage that a "busy life is a deep and meaningful life." And so, we busy ourselves with what we see as appropriate; serving God by doing as much as possible *for time is short and who knows how long we have?* We think we must maximize every moment, making the most of every opportunity.

But our faith life is shallow. There is nothing solid on which to stand. A small squall breaks out and we crumble under its slight pressure. What happened to all our words of faith that we so confidently proclaimed during our acts of service?

They were only words, that's what. Abel understood this, and so did David. The second-born of the first man knew the heart of God desired the richest and best part of the animal he chose for sacrifice. Out of devotion to God and in a desire to please Him, Abel gave the fat portion because he knew it pleased God. This best part rightfully belonged to God anyway, but Abel recognized this truth and willingly gave it back to Him in sacrifice.

Later in the history of man's quest to live uprightly in the world God created, came one who also chose well. This shepherd boy who had captured the heart of God knew that his best for God existed entirely within his own heart. His brokenness over his own sin, such deep sorrow over how he grieved God in his transgressions that he was willing to let those fleshly desires go and turn completely away from them, was the best that God was looking for from him. David knew a broken and contrite spirit is deemed to be our best offering to Him.

And so, it is our attitude, our willingness to give this best to God, the fat portions so to speak, that sets the standard by which to live that Jesus makes possible for us. Our best is not measured quantitatively. It is not about how much we do or how often we serve or even how willing we are to say "yes" every time we are asked. Instead, our best is measured in the heart where a willingness to place ourselves in the hands of God as a living sacrifice is what is deemed as acceptable to Him (Romans 12:1). This form of worship is an act of sacred service to God, an offering of our best to Him. The decisions we make, the paths we follow, the way we look at life; these can all potentially honor God as a good and acceptable offering when we are willing to yield to His best for us. It is so much better than trying to impress God with exuberance or serving out of obligation or guilt, or killing ourselves by trying to keep busy for God.

God knows our heart. He doesn't care if we spend every waking moment serving Him in the way we see fit. What He really is pleased with is a heart submitted to Him and His will for our lives. This is the better offering that will set our Father's heart to singing!

> *If worship is just one thing we do,*
> *everything becomes mundane.*
> *If worship is the one thing we do,*
> *everything takes on eternal significance.*
> —Timothy J. Christenson

How do you give God the leftovers of your heart, failing to let Him have His way in the deepest part of you?

When do you try hard to do what you think is right without ever considering what He really wants from you: your humble repentance?

How do you work hard for God without even desiring to know Him and draw closer to Him?

Heavenly Father,

I admit I often have it backwards, thinking I can earn Your good graces or that I must constantly work to earn my keep and make You pleased. In reality, I already have Your grace, security in Your family and Your pleasure through Christ, if only I would nail on the cross the sin I often cling to like a comforting teddy bear. When I honestly see how much it offends You when I act like I have no other choice than to fall into sin when Jesus died to deliver freedom from this sin, I have won Your heart with my brokenness. And this humble act of remorse and sorrow over my sin, coupled with a willingness to turn away from it and grasp Your best for me, pleases You to no end. You'd rather I spend a day sitting at Your feet in humble adoration than a thousand attempting to give You any less. Help me to worship You with such an offering as this.

In Jesus' name I pray, Amen

40

How to Please God

"By faith Enoch was taken from this life, so that he did not experience death: 'He could not be found, because God had taken him away.' For before he was taken, he was commended as one who pleased God. And without faith it is impossible to please God, because anyone who come to him must believe that he exists and that he rewards those who earnestly seek him" (Hebrews 11:5-6).

As a child, I always wanted to please my mother but never really knew how. I tried jumping through hoops, doing whatever she asked, going above and beyond what was necessary, getting good grades. Since she was not aware of my yearning to impress her with my performance, my mother didn't ever let me know if I was exceeding her expectations. After all, she wasn't a mind-reader, just a plain ole mom.

Thankfully, I don't have to put myself through such efforts to try to please God because He has let us know through the life of Enoch what delights Him. He loves it when we use our entire beings, our spirit that gives us the ability to feel, think and decide, to live in communion with His Spirit. Another way to put it is He wants us to walk by the Spirit of God, to worship Him in spirit and truth, to seek Him with all our hearts. No matter how you say it, it comes down to being "all in." To completely buy what God is selling, to fully place our trust in Him, to desire a life connected to him every step of the way means to follow Him wherever He may lead.

This seems to be the kind of life Enoch led. This father of the oldest man ever recorded walked "in close fellowship with God" (Genesis 5:24 NLT). It was Enoch's habit to fellowship with God, like a man with a good friend. He didn't merely believe God existed, but he took it a step further. He cherished the bond he shared with God.

What does this look like? Well, for one it meant he saw God as someone who could be known, who he could spend time with. It reminds me of my best friend when I was eleven. Denise lived around the corner and we spent a lot of time together. I remember telling my mom that I wished I could live with her because I never grew tired of her company. I felt a close bond, at least for a time, with this friend. This is kind of how Enoch related to God: He loved Him and couldn't get enough of His company.

The other aspect of this faith that pleases God is that it concerns our hearts. Enoch seemed to model this heart-centered faith; he was bent on pursuing God. And the thing about God is that He's easy to find. He's not an enigma who cloaks Himself in mystery and shadows so that only the most obsessed, righteous searchers can find Him. He is a God who wants to be found, who longs for relationship with the people He has created, who loves to walk in the garden in the cool of the day with His image-bearers. Sometimes, though, we don't want to be found. We feel ashamed or unworthy or unfit for such a relationship. Faith, though, reminds us that Jesus came to make a way to this vital relationship, to cover our estranging sin with His blood so we can boldly approach the throne of grace. God-pleasing faith passionately and without reserve runs after Him, knowing He wants nothing more than our company.

So how do we please God? We go further than simple belief that God exists. We live like Enoch who faithfully spent time with God, longing for more and more of Him as the days went by, and pursuing Him with all our hearts with a hunger that only He can quench. In short, we please God when we desire nothing more than to grow closer in our relationship with Him.

Develop a heart that can't get enough of His company,
and know that He wants nothing more
than our full attentions.
This is the kind of faith that pleases God.

When do you try to please God by what you do instead of how you relate to Him?

_____

_____

How do you fall into the trap of trying to earn your way into God's presence?

Heavenly Father,

I love You and want to please You more than anything, but I often think this involves meeting expectations I have set, or reaching standards that are impossible for me to reach. Help me to desire more of You each day, seeing that Jesus made it possible for me to freely come to You, and knowing that You want this more than anything, I want to seek You wholeheartedly. I desire You and vow to walk faithfully with You just as Enoch did, for I know this is what You want from me.
In Jesus' Name I pray, Amen

41
Unfathomable Promise

"By faith Noah, when warned about things not yet seen, in holy fear built an ark to save his family. By his faith he condemned the world and became heir of the righteousness that is in keeping with faith" (Hebrews 11:7).

What if God told you that in a few years the earth would enter a worm hole where it would travel by the speed of light to another galaxy? As incredible as this warning is, let's say it's not the entire content of the message. What if God also said that no human would be able to endure such a trip and the only way for you and your family to survive is to build a special vessel custom made to hold you and a pair of every species of animal existing on earth? Would you believe Him? Would you obey His command and build an enormous space vessel that could sustain such a journey? Or would you ignore Him and hope He was just kidding or that you were imagining things?

Perhaps this ludicrous scenario gives us an idea of what it was like for Noah. In the hundreds of years since God had created the earth, no one had ever seen rain. While drops of water falling from the sky is a normal thing for us, no one had experienced rain until roughly 2,300 B.C. when God flooded the earth with water that both gushed forth from underground storehouses and downpoured from the sky.

It would have taken great faith for Noah to trust God that this strange thing would happen just as He said, and even greater faith for Noah to spend dozens of years working hard to complete the ark according to God's explicit instructions. There is no doubt that Noah possessed a strong faith in God.

While God may not be warning us of such a fantastical happening as a world-wide flood, or a cosmic journey through a worm-hole for that matter, He does test our faith in ways that make it hard to trust Him. He allows circumstances into our lives that push us beyond our abilities and makes us wonder if the trials and tribulations are worth it. He places us in situations where we are out on a limb, looking like fools compared to the rest of the world so that our faith will be proven as real when we stand firm, not caving into peer pressure or giving up in an effort to fit in with everyone else. He sometimes even places us in harm's way where others wonder why we would take such a risk, not understanding our faith in God's unfailing plan and our quest for His glory above all things.

In these situations, we will be called "goody-two-shoes" and accused of thinking of ourselves as better than everyone else. Like Noah, our decision to walk the path of life makes those who reject the Truth look bad in comparison. But like Noah, we are not better, just better off by faith. In other words, our decision to risk sticking out like a sore thumb in order to follow the teachings of a God we've never seen who is claiming things we can only hope will come to pass, will earn for us a right standing with God by faith.

Just like Noah, our decision to take God at His Word and believe Jesus as the only way to be made right with God will result in a righteousness that comes by this faith. If we doubt, however, we'll end up thinking we're not good enough, or that we must earn our way to God, or that there is something more we must do in addition to what Jesus has already mercifully done. Either we believe God and let the ark that is Jesus save us, or we die along with all the others who reject such a gracious offer. The ticket to board the ark of rescue from condemnation is faith in Jesus, pure and simple.

The faith of Noah meant believing God as He warned of something yet unseen. The faith of modern man means trusting God as He warns of tragedy yet to come and not proven as true. Either way, it takes faith to be saved.

Either you will take God at His Word and be saved,
Or you will reject His unfathomable promise and be lost.

Just because the Gospel is hard to believe, or sounds too good to be true, do you reject it as fantasy or an impossibility?

_____

_____

When do you think you can't be saved? That you are too far gone or beyond saving?

_____

_____

How do you doubt in God's ability to do as He has said and love you just as you are?

_____

_____

Heavenly Father,

I hear the Gospel message, that You sent Jesus to take my place in the punishment of death so that I could live an abundant life that will last forever, and I wonder if it could be true. I've never seen Heaven, making it hard to believe there is such a place. Give me the faith of Noah, who took your Word at face value, believing even though he'd never witnessed of what You warned him. Help me to trust You at Your Word.

In Jesus' Name I pray, Amen

42
Looking Forward

"By faith Abraham, when called to go to a place he would later receive as his inheritance, obeyed and went, even though he did not know where he was going. By faith he made his home in the promised land like a stranger in a foreign country; he lived in tents, as did Isaac and Jacob, who were heirs with him of the same promise. For he was looking forward to the city with foundations, whose architect and builder is God" (Hebrews 11:8-10).

When I go on a road trip, I like to have a map. I enjoy looking at all the interesting places we will pass through in a day, but mostly I like to know where we are going. I want to know where I am each moment as well as our destination and when we will arrive. I like maps because they help me feel like I'm in control of where I'm headed, how I'll get there and the timetable of the trip.

Abraham didn't have such a hang up. He was willing to pack up his belongings, heading out on a trek with all his animals, servants, nephew, and his family, as well as his beloved wife without even knowing where they would end up. He didn't know the route they would take, the ETA or even the purpose for such a trip. All Abraham knew was that God said to go and that was enough for him to hit the road. And then, when he finally got to the land God had promised him, it wasn't even technically his. So, he had to set up a temporary home, continuing to live as a nomad even though God said the land would be his.

What if we lived with such faith? Instead of needing to know all the details before following God's lead, we'd just step out without asking a single question, simply based on the fact that God had called us. When He prompts us to give all our savings to a family in need, we would do so, believing that God has a plan to take care of our own needs and is the One who provides financial security, not our healthy bank account. Or when He places a burden on our heart to adopt an orphan, we would obey without wondering how we'll feed an extra mouth or find the emotional resources to love a hurting child or handle the responsibilities of such a commitment. Or when He inspires us to sell everything we have and move across the country to care for the needs of a loved one, we would do it without fearing the loss of beloved objects, good friends and familiar surroundings or worrying about how we'll manage once there.

The faith of Abraham trusts without expecting to see the big picture God is painting. The faith of Abraham hands over to God the responsibility of navigation on the journey of life. The faith of Abraham doesn't expect to live in physically lavish surroundings, knowing the good stuff is yet to come.

Faith is going without knowing,
And following without seeing.
How do you expect to know all the details of a calling
before you'll take one step in obedience?

_____

_____

When do you only trust what you can see or even what
you can imagine yourself doing?

_____

_____

How do you limit God's work in your life by your
unbelief?

_____

_____

Heavenly Father,
*   I am grateful that You include me in Your great plan,*
wanting to use me to further Your purposes. Help me to
trust You as Abraham did, without knowing the what,
when, where, why, and how. Help me to simply be
satisfied with the who: You! May my knowledge of Your
sovereign power be enough to spur me forward in

obedience, trusting that You'll direct my footsteps and empower me every step of the way.
In Jesus' Name I pray, Amen

43
Small Faith Can be Great Faith

"And by faith even Sarah, who was past child-bearing age, was enabled to bear children because she considered him faithful who had made the promise. And so from this one man, and he as good as dead, came descendants as numerous as the stars in the sky and as countless as the sand on the seashore" (Hebrews 11:11-12).

It was what she had always wanted. What was it to be a woman if she didn't have children to care for, to give her heart to, to carry on her legacy? In her society, a barren woman such as herself was less than whole. At her age, though, she wondered: *was it possible? could she still become a mother?* God had promised that this time next year she would bear a child, but she had never seen anyone in her ninth decade raise a baby, let alone deliver one. She had come to a peace within herself that she may never taste the joys of motherhood, a kind of acceptance of what seemed inevitable. Still, there was that glimmer of hope that this God her husband trusted, and whom she herself believed to be faithful, would follow through and do as He said He would do.

Sometimes our faith is not the strongest. We may feel we are no Moses, David or Deborah so maybe we wouldn't make it into the Hall of Fame of Faith. After all, we're no pillar of conviction, no stalwart beacon of devotion to God, no example of how to trust God through all the ups and downs of life. We've had periods of doubt, moments of questioning, entire blocks of time when we wondered if this faith in God thing was all it's cracked up to be.

Faith is still faith, no matter how big or small, and it all counts. Even the smallest act done by faith in a big God gives us His approval or is credited to us as righteousness. Jesus said, ". . . if you have faith as small as a mustard seed, you can say to this mountain, 'Move from here to there,' and it will move" (Matthew 17:20). It's not the size of our faith that counts, but the genuine quality and the faithfulness of the object of that faith that matters.

So, even though Sarah doubted, laughing to herself when she considered the pledge from God Himself that she would deliver a child at the age of ninety, she did carry a measure of assurance that what He said would happen would indeed come to pass. She passes on to us the guarantee that even a glimmer of hope in a God of the unseen counts in God's book. As a result, let's hang onto the faith we have, believing in a God who has proved Himself as worthy of our trust.

This means there is no shame in doubt, nor does our questioning cancel out what little faith we have. Instead, it only fortifies the fact that our lack of faith does not, by one iota, nullify God's faithfulness. In other words, our inability to trust God at all times does not label Him as One who can't be trusted, nor does it minimize His dependability. Instead, it only shows our own weaknesses and thus our need for a Lord who can increase our faith.

What do we struggle to believe? What seems impossible, out of the realm of natural occurrences or beyond the time constraints of normal existence? What do you doubt could really happen but deep down in the recesses of your heart, you hold out a glimmer of hope that maybe, just perhaps, this impossible thing could be accomplished by a God of the impossible? Does this itty-bitty faith count as faith? Or is it seen more as skepticism, disbelief or even mistrust? Sarah's example leaves behind for us the hope that even a little bit of faith is enough to earn for us an entry into the Hall of Fame of Faith. God is not impressed with the scope of our faith, just the fact that there is evidence of some at all.

It's not the amount of faith that matters,
but the sincerity of our trust in a God
who can take even the smallest confidence
in Him and use it to move mountains.

How do you discount your tiny faith as negligible in the scheme of things, thinking your doubt or fear outweighs what little trust in God you have?

How would it comfort you to know that God does not look down on your doubt, but he truly honors your faith in Him, no matter how small or fleeting?

_____

_____

Heavenly Father,

I am thankful that my place in Your family is not based on the size of my faith, but simply in its sincerity. Help me to trust You more each day, realizing that I can't lose Your love no matter how often I doubt or fail to trust You with day-to-day issues. Give me the peace that comes from realizing that my identity in You is secure. I love You and am so thankful for Your grace and mercy which abounds in my life, even when I'm doubting or wondering about the feasibility of Your promises. Help me to trust You more each day.

In Jesus' Name I pray, Amen.

44
Eternity Focused

"All these people were still living by faith when they died. They did not receive the things promised; they only saw them and welcomed them from a distance, admitting that they were foreigners and strangers on earth. People who say such things show that they are looking for a country of their own. If they had been thinking of the country they had left, they would have had opportunity to return. Instead, they were longing for a better country—a heavenly one. Therefore God is not ashamed to be called their God, for he has prepared a city for them" (Hebrews 11:13-16).

"If I don't get it, I'm going to give up. I've worked too hard and waited too long to walk away empty-handed!" Does this sound familiar? Many of us have fought for something long and hard, whether it be human rights, a promotion, respect, or even a prized possession. Whatever the "it" is, we all understand the concept of getting what we've hoped for.

God's kingdom has a different economy from this worldly mindset. Our flesh assumes faith is rewarded with receiving what was hoped for. If we believe we'll be healed from the cancer that plagues us, then our faith will be rewarded with healing. If we trust that God will repair our marriage, then our faith will bring about reconciliation. If we never falter in our confidence that God will give us children, then our faith will bring about fertility. Sometimes it doesn't turn out that way, though, and it's not because we wavered in our faith.

Perhaps faith is more than just getting what we're hoping for. This passage suggests that faith is something greater than receiving what we believe we'll get. Rather than just a method to place our requests to a Santa-like God who then gauges the strength and veracity of our faith and grants wishes accordingly. It is more about the next world than this. In other words, the great men and women of faith who are recorded in this chapter were hoping for something here on earth. But more than that, they were looking forward to what was to come, knowing that it would be far better than anything received in the here and now.

So while we can trust God to deliver, our eternity-focused heart will yearn for more than only the temporal deliverance found here. What is hoped for in this life dims to what we believe is coming in the next. So, this exercise of faith is less about receiving and more about growing in our ability to trust God no matter how things turn out. This test of faith is based on whether we keep believing even when we don't get what we expect, knowing our true reward is yet to come. As we continue to grow in our faith, it becomes more and more evident that heavenly blessings are more valuable than earthly ones, the future highly prized compared to the present.

Praying for healing is a godly thing, but placing our hope in the new, perfect body that will be delivered in eternity is what gives us strength to carry on through the treatments. Believing in the restoration of a marital relationship is a good thing, but knowing that true peace and reconciliation will happen in Heaven is what helps us carry on no matter the outcome. Trusting in God for the blessing of children is a wonderful hope, but realizing the fulfillment of every desire that will come in our Father's house keeps us going even if we don't experience the joys of child rearing here.

Faith is more than just receiving what we hope for, but it is learning to look forward to our eternal hope in Jesus. What is to come is far greater than anything we can have here. May that spur us on to greater faith.

Faith in receiving what we want now is good,
But faith in what is to come is even greater!

How do you base your faith on whether or not you receive what you are waiting for?

_____

_____

When do you waver in your faith if you have to wait a long time?

_____

_____

Heavenly Father,

    I know You have my best interests at heart, but more than that, I know what is to come is greater than anything You can give me now. Help me to base my trust in You, on who You are, not on what I'll get out of the relationship. Help me to have faith in what You have promised in eternity more than on what I must look forward to here on earth. Grant me Your economy so I value eternal blessings more than the temporal that often draw me so strongly. In Jesus' Name I pray, Amen

45

Greater in the Unseen

"By faith he (Moses) left Egypt, not fearing the king's anger; he persevered because he saw him who is invisible" (Hebrews 11:27).

They had been under his thumb all their lives. His harsh rule was the only leadership they had ever known. The crack of his whip on their backs and the revenge sought against them by his powerful hand was their reality. The edicts passed down that threatened their livelihood, their well-being, the sanctity of their families, and their very lives was something they were used to. The Israelites didn't like being slaves in Egypt, but it was their lot in life. And because of their position, they knew only too well the wrath of Pharaoh.

So when the time came to flee, to take the opening offered by this emotionally unstable man who ruled Egypt, it was not an easy thing. It was like an American slave fleeing the obsessed and possessive master, or a battered woman getting out from under her violent and mentally disturbed husband. They knew the rage their flight would incite in their oppressor. They were personally familiar with the ways he would get back at them. They were not ignorant of the danger they were putting themselves in. Even though Pharaoh commanded them to leave in a moment of fearful horror at the loss of his own firstborn son and the dread of what else this God may do, the people of Israel realized that he could change his mind.

Instead of wavering in their faith, however, Moses led the people of God to do exactly as God had instructed. For that moment in time, they could see the unseen God more clearly than the king who had tormented them for so long. They believed that God Almighty was so much more powerful than this tyrant they'd grown up fearing. It was clear to them that greater was the One who led them from above than the one who oppressed them from below. And so they obeyed.

Perhaps it was the impressive demonstration of His might in striking down the firstborn of every household in Egypt. Or it could have been the realization of their own salvation from a similar fate as the wails of their oppressors reminded them of the favor of God that was theirs and the blood of the lamb that protected them. Or maybe it was simple faith bolstered after the intimacy with their God in the institution of the first Passover celebration. Whatever it was, they believed the word of God enough to do as He had said.

What is it that strikes fear in our hearts, blocking our view of the all-powerful God? Sometimes we are afraid to step forward into the inky unknown, dreading what lurks in the darkness more than we trust in the God whose light overpowers even the blackest of nights. Other times we are more worried about how our obedience to God's calling will affect our standing in society, undermining all we've worked for, forgetting it is His opinion that matters most and that our place in His family is eternally secure no matter how hard this life gets. There are even times when we resist His leading due to the panic that grips our hearts when we think of all we could lose, overlooking the fact that we are building treasures in Heaven that can never be lost.

In order to walk by faith, we must always look through a lense of faith that allow us to see what is invisible to the naked eye. When we do, we will never fail to see the enormity of the God who is for us. With Him at our side, what is there to fear?

Fear knocked at the door.
Faith answered.
No one was there.

How often do you fail to see the power that is in you through faith in Jesus Christ who gives you the strength to persevere?

_____

_____

When do you assume life is what you make of it and that the outcome is dependent upon everything that is visible and understood by you?

_____

_____

Could you admit there is a spiritual realm where supernatural work occurs on your behalf by an invisible God who loves you?

_____

_____

How do you dismiss the real power that comes from God by placing all your trust in the inferior power that is from what you can see, touch, and comprehend?

_____

_____

Heavenly Father,

Thank You for not giving up on me. I so often fail to see You even though You have never left my side. Help me to remember that just because my physical eyes cannot detect Your presence doesn't mean You aren't there, always at work on my behalf. Give me spiritual lenses to see the might of Your presence, and may it spur me on to obedience to You.

In Jesus' Name I pray, Amen.

46
Run the Race of Jesus

"Therefore, since we are surrounded by such a great cloud of witnesses, let us throw off everything that hinders and the sin that so easily entangles. And let us run with perseverance the race marked out for us, fixing our eyes on Jesus, the pioneer and perfecter of faith. For the joy set before him he endured the cross, scorning its shame, and sat down at the right hand of the throne of God. Consider him who endured such opposition from sinners, so that you will not grow weary and lose heart" (Hebrews 12:1-4).

During His three-year ministry, powerful men were constantly opposing Him. It was rare for Him to teach without raising the ire of church leaders who thought themselves in the position to do damage to His reputation or to stop the momentum of His following. Some of His most life-changing miracles were seen as an affront to God and His law, and even loving acts were painted as being hostile to God. He just couldn't win.

Then came the point when all this planning and scheming by the powers-that-be came to a head. He agonized over what was to come; the torture, the scorning, the shaming, the pain, but mostly the separation from His Father and the enduring of His righteous, holy wrath. His Spirit desired nothing more than to obey but His flesh knew the price He'd pay to step forward in submission. His innocence was declared guilty, His pure goodness was placed in the hands of evil, He who knew no sin became sin. Then it was finished; He had paid the ultimate price.

How did Jesus endure such hostility? It's not that He was God so of course He was able to get through it. No. Let's not minimize His suffering, His sacrifice. As a human made of flesh, He was fully man. He had set aside His divinity while He resided on earth as a mere mortal. He suffered as any man would. He was tempted like you and I are. He struggled to obey, just like us. Still, He persevered. He kept walking the path meant for Him. He never caved into the pressure to conform to the world or ease His own pain. It was hard for Him to live a perfect life, but He did it. And it cost Him much humiliation, pain, suffering, and loneliness. No, He didn't persevere because it was somehow easy for Him as a God-Man.

So how was He able to endure such hostility, such torture, such abandonment? He kept His eyes on the prize. He never forgot His true place at the right hand of His Father, never failed to keep in mind His destination. He was spurred on by remembering from where He came and to where He was headed. He knew this horrible nightmare was temporary, and soon it would end.

Jesus' mindset and focus can help us as we face temptation to give in to what comes naturally to our flesh, or when we are treated like an outlaw even though we are innocent, or when we feel oh-so alone, abandoned by everyone we thought cared for us or are lacking in meaningful human connection. We can do as Jesus did and keep our eyes on where we are headed in eternity, giving us courage to continue placing one foot in front of another. We can also keep from giving up by remembering all Jesus endured for us, and realizing we are empowered by His Spirit. He is more than our example; He is our destiny, the gateway through which we enter His Kingdom in the here and now.

It is His empowering blood that gives us hope for tomorrow. The place He is preparing for us gives us courage to press on no matter how many times we fall, no matter how often we are attacked, or how bad life seems. After all, we haven't struggled so hard as to have lost our life. In this way, Jesus helps to keep our journey of faith in perspective. It is by remembering His life, death and resurrection that we have the courage to continue and the vision of what we look forward to. And this is how we run the race set before us, just as Jesus did, for it's not really our race, but His.

We have hope,
and His name is Jesus.

How are you feeling sorry for yourself in the difficult times you now face, forgetting that Jesus' lot in His life here on earth was far worse?

_____

_____

When do you lose sight of where you are headed in eternity?

_____

_____

How can remembering what you have to look forward to help you endure the hard times now, or even to stand firm against the temptations that lure you?

_____

_____

Heavenly Father,

Jesus is my example, but more than that, He is the hope I have in living this life You've called me to live. In Him, I have the power to withstand temptation but also the anticipation of my eternal home where all my desires will be met and my deepest longings fulfilled. It is this that can give me the courage to withstand the treatment I now face. It is the sight of Jesus enduring far worse that puts my current situation in perspective. Without Jesus, I have no hope, nor do I have the power to live. And so, I give thanks for Jesus, the Author and Perfecter of my faith.
In Jesus' Name I pray, Amen

47

Trouble or Discipline?

"Endure hardship as discipline; God is treating you as his children. For what children are not disciplined by their father? If you are not disciplined—and everyone undergoes discipline— then you are not legitimate, not true sons and daughters at all. Moreover, we have all had human fathers who disciplined us and we respected them for it. How much more should we submit to the Father of spirits and live! They disciplined us for a little while as they thought best; but God disciplines us for our good, in order that we may share in his holiness. No discipline seems pleasant at the time, but painful. Later, however, it produces a harvest of righteousness and peace for those who have been trained by it" (Hebrews 12:7-11).

He was born on the streets with his sister. The only mentality he knew was a fend-for-yourself kind of approach, scrapping for tidbits of food and often running for his life. Every human was a threat and he trusted no one. Then he was rescued. This beautiful orange tabby cat with the white socks and bib was adopted into our family. Unfortunately, because of his feral nature, it was hard to get a good look at Kale let alone pet him. Over the years, he grew more comfortable with us but still mostly maintained his wild nature.

Then our family went through a series of heartbreaking losses. First his litter mate lost her life to a sudden lung infection, then the "elder statesman" who presided over the brood finally succumbed to death after nineteen years of life. Finally, possibly the most shocking loss of all, was the sudden heart attack of his best buddy whom we found dead one evening with no warning signs at all. With each tragedy, Kale, the lone survivor, seemed to grow stronger. Each blow only served to stretch him in inexplicable ways until he began acting like a normal cat. He became comfortable with our two dogs, enjoyed long rub downs, cuddled on the bed with his human family, and seemed to completely lose his skittishness. Kale seemed the better for all the loss he had suffered.

Kale's example reminds me of how God uses the hard stuff, the tragedies, the hardships to correct our wrong behavior, to curb our passions, to grow our faith, until we suddenly find ourselves to be inexplicitly changed from the inside out. This loving yet firm hand of our Father who guides us through disciplinary action is meant to grow us into the men and women He created us to be. This seemingly harsh treatment is evidence that we belong to Him, that He cares enough to not just leave us as we are, but to create wake-up calls to draw us back to Him, to design difficult terrain for us to negotiate which will purge the unnecessary baggage from our possession, and to teach us His better way of living. Without these life-lessons we would only stay as we are, stuck in our hopeless ways, kind of like the way Kale was all those years, living as a feral cat in a domestic situation. The hard losses purged all the fear from him and now he is enjoying life as he was meant to live it.

Just like Kale was content in his fearful ways, we are also stuck in sinful strongholds, or have developed unhealthy patterns, or our pride is manifesting in ways that promotes self-centeredness instead of God-focus. So He gets to work with hammer and chisel, painfully breaking away all that is needless, and carefully, lovingly shapes us as He desires us to be. If He didn't love us as children, He would leave us as we are. If we were estranged from Him, as illegitimate children, he would give us over to our own devices.

But as we are, we have been bought at a price, redeemed from illegitimacy by the blood of Jesus, ushered into a world-wide, eternal family with God as our Father and Jesus as our Brother. And so, we are loved enough to bear the discipline of a true son or daughter. So let us praise God today for His firm yet loving hand of correction and His kindly, expert artists' eye. For us, hardships may appear as if God is trying to make our lives difficult, but in reality, it's more of a sign of His lovingkindness to refuse to leave us as we are. For this, we can give thanks to Him.

It's not just trouble,
It's discipline.

How do I look at hard times as nothing but suffering instead of seeing it as a sign that God is teaching me something?

When am I resistant to the lessons He's trying to teach me?

Heavenly Father,

I am thankful to be yours and I know a part of living as your child is that I must undergo discipline. I am not perfect, and there is much growth and transformation I must endure. Help me to see this as a sweet sign of my inclusion in Your family, of Your lovingkindness to me as Your child, instead of only viewing the hard times as drudgery and torture. You have my best interest at heart, so I have nothing to fear!

In Jesus' Name I pray, Amen

48
Battle Buddy Mentality

"Make every effort to live in peace with everyone and to be holy; without holiness no one will see the Lord. See to it that no one falls short of the grace of God and that no bitter root grows up to cause trouble and defile many. See that no one is sexually immoral, or is godless like Esau, who for a single meal sold his inheritance rights as the oldest son. Afterward, as you know, when he wanted to inherit this blessing he was rejected. Even though he sought the blessing with tears, he could not change what he had done" (Hebrews 12:14-17).

We are used to being responsible for our own actions, for living our own lives, for being accountable to none but ourselves. If we make a mess of our lives, we figure we have no one to blame but ourselves, and if things go well, it follows that we get all the credit for a job well done. God's kingdom is designed differently than this. In fact, relationship is so important to God that He desires us to build strong bonds with each other and to live in genuine community with His family. It turns out that this means more than just breaking bread or studying God's Word together. There is more to this community than just hanging out with one another, and this godly perspective makes most of us highly uncomfortable, but also makes us stronger.

God wants us to get personal with each other. He wants us to hold each other accountable; to be vigilant when it comes to rooting out the source of dissension within the family, and to make sure that we are all on track in the sanctification process. He wants us to stay close to the course God has marked out for us, making sure we all are completely dependent upon His grace and not falling back on our own merits or efforts. While I'd rather keep to myself and mind my own business, there is a reason we are our brothers' keepers.

Since we as sinful beings are bent on destructive ways and we don't always see things clearly, we must help each other stay on track, be committed to building each other up and strengthening bonds, and to encourage Christ-centered living and discourage the natural drift toward self-centeredness.

While our relationship with Christ is a personal one, we do not exist in a vacuum, nor are we the Lone Ranger, meant to struggle through on our own. Instead, we are meant to lean on one another, bear one another's burdens and be willingly to speak the truth in love to restore healthy fellowship. It is not enough just to wonder why a brother or sister has succumbed to temptation, but to do whatever is necessary to lovingly restore them. It's easy to be blinded by sin, and we need to support each other as battle buddies do, holding each other accountable so that in the end, we will not be begging for the blessing we rejected in our self-centered weakness.

In combat, soldiers in the U.S. Army are encouraged to look out for one another with the belief that the unit is only as strong as their weakest link. Part of this responsibility is for each battle buddy to assess the emotional well-being of his partner, especially in combat situations. If suicidal or distressed feelings are detected, they are encouraged to take actions to prevent their buddy from ending their own lives or sabotaging the mission, and advocating for them until they are strong enough to do so for themselves. In this way, the whole is strengthened one piece at a time.

Similarly, the Body of Christ is made up of many parts in one body and we are connected together by an eternal bond through faith in Christ. It is designed so that if one suffers, we all suffer. If one rejoices, it is a celebration to be experienced by the whole. Therefore, we must think as a soldier does and look out for one another, assessing the emotional and spiritual health of our brothers and sisters. Not only is it in our best interest that we do so, but it is our call as a holy nation, lest we turn to trouble and vagrancy. We have a family so let's act like one by caring enough to live as one.

The life of faith is not a solitary one,
but a group effort
with Christ as the head,
the Spirit as our power,
to the glory of our Father.

How do you try to go it alone, resisting the gentle probing of your brother or sister as they attempt to challenge you in your walk?

_____

_____

When are you threatened by a challenging question instead of seeing it as the loving intervention that it is?

_____

_____

Where are you resisting the group effort meant to draw you closer to the Head that is Christ?

_____

_____

Heavenly Father,

I admit that I tend to want to go it alone, live a solitary life or at least keep my problems to myself. But You have designed me to live in community where I will be treasured but also challenged so that I will not let my flesh have its way in my life. My brothers and sisters are here to love me, and sometimes that love means exhorting me to stay the path and cease from straying. Give me the humility to accept such counsel as the loving act it is, for Your glory. In Jesus' Name I pray, Amen

49
The Greatest Gift of All

"You have not come to a mountain that can be touched and that is burning with fire; to darkness, gloom and storm; to a trumpet blast or to such a voice speaking words that those who heard it begged that no further word be spoken to them, because they could not bear what was commanded: 'If even an animal touches the mountain, it must be stoned to death.' The sight was so terrifying that Moses said, 'I am trembling with fear.'

But you have come to Mount Zion, to the city of the living God, the heavenly Jerusalem. You have come to thousands upon thousands of angels in joyful assembly, to the church of the firstborn, whose names are written in heaven. You have come to God, the Judge of all, to the spirits of the righteous made perfect, to Jesus the mediator of a new covenant, and to the sprinkled blood that speaks a better word than the blood of Abel" (Hebrews 12:18-24).

I used to be afraid to go near. I didn't know them, opting to merely watch from afar. I thought it would be nice to be close like the other kids, but I just didn't feel like I belonged. *Maybe someday they will invite me to join in the fun.*

Have you ever felt like you were on the outside looking in? Barred from enjoying all the good things those on the "inside" seem so comfortable doing? It happens often enough in life, and no one likes to feel left out. When it comes to God, though, being on the outside is not just an uncomfortable or sad thing. Being on the wrong side of God has serious, eternal ramifications.

We often hear about the love of God, the grace of God, and the mercy of God. We hear how He left the ninety-nine to seek out the one who strayed. We know He is slow to anger. These are the attributes of God we love to hear about, and every one of them are absolutely true. There is, however, another side of God. Part of His character is His holiness, which sets Him apart and above all things. He is just, always judging rightly. He is righteous, never doing wrong and always doing right. When you combine these three together, you find that He is unable to look past sin and forgive, letting it go merely out of the goodness of His heart. No, there is no forgiveness without the shedding of blood (Hebrews 9:22). Sin must be dealt with as it rightfully earns His judgement and thus His wrath. This is bad news for us as it leaves us on the outside looking in.

Love and holiness, grace and justice, mercy and righteousness; only Jesus could reconcile such diametrically opposed characteristics of God. Only He could demonstrate His love through the sacrifice of His only Son as a sin offering, holy and pleasing to Him. Only He could satisfy the righteousness so that mercy could be delivered to a guilty people. Only He who knew no sin could graciously become sin for us so that we could receive the forgiveness of sins we could never earn. And in so doing, Christ reconciled us with the Judge who held our fate in His Holy Hands.

Under the covering of the perfect blood of Christ shed for us, we are given the right to be transformed from enemy-combatant to cherished child and are thus invited to Mount Zion where all who are forgiven by the blood of the Lamb will assemble to joyfully worship Him. And it is here where we may dwell in His Presence, the greatest gift of all, from now until all eternity. Once awakened to His goodness, nothing else will do, as pastor and author Henry Blackaby notes, "You will never be satisfied just to know *about* God. Really knowing God only comes through experiences as He reveals Himself to you." And in a heartbeat, by faith in Christ, you are on the inside.

The blood of Jesus removes the fear
we have of God as Judge
and replaces it with the love
we were meant to have of God as Father.

Have you thought about the perfect holiness of God and how your eternal fate lies in His hands? Have you accepted His offer of salvation and eternal life only available through faith in the cross of Christ and sub-mission to His lordship over your life?

_____

_____

Are you at peace with God?

_____

_____

Heavenly Father,

I worship and praise You as the holy God who rightfully can judge me as a rebel at heart. I am grateful for the grace and mercy shown to me on the cross when Jesus bore my sins upon His own perfect body. Help me to remember the peace I now enjoy with You so that I can come to You as a cherished child instead of as Your enemy and the worst of all sinners. May I take advantage of the invitation You extend to me to draw close to You so that our intimacy and bond may grow. Nothing else will quench the deep thirst I have for You. Thank you for sending Your Son to make this possible.

In Jesus' Name I pray, Amen

50
Joyful Reverence

"You have not come to a mountain that can be touched and that is burning with fire; to darkness, gloom and storm; to a trumpet blast or to such a voice speaking words that those who heard it begged that no further word be spoken to them, because they could not bear what was commanded: 'If even an animal touches the mountain, it must be stoned to death.' The sight was so terrifying that Moses said, 'I am trembling with fear.'

But you have come to Mount Zion, to the city of the living God, the heavenly Jerusalem. You have come to thousands upon thousands of angels in joyful assembly, to the church of the firstborn, whose names are written in heaven. You have come to God, the Judge of all, to the spirits of the righteous made perfect, to Jesus the mediator of a new covenant, and to the sprinkled blood that speaks a better word than the blood of Abel" (Hebrews 12:18-24).

It was terrifying to think about. There was no way to get around this Judge, no way to sweet-talk our way into His good graces, no loophole of which to take advantage. This Judge is perfectly righteous and completely intolerant of sin. One slip and we're doomed. Unfortunately, we're all condemned because there is none righteous, not even one.

Then enters the Mediator into the courtroom, the Go-between, the Conduit of mercy who did the unthinkable, standing between us and the Dispenser of Justice. He bore the wrath of the Righteous One whose death sentence we deserved. When He stepped in our stead, He took the punishment upon Himself. Instead of wrath and judgement, we now by faith through grace receive forgiveness and the righteousness of God. Instead of hanging back for fear of being struck down by a holy God, we can freely come forward and assemble with joy. Our terror at being found out is replaced by a gladness of being accepted as worthy.

God is both righteous and merciful, holy and gracious, just and forgiving. One cannot be denied in recognition of the other. He cannot dispense mercy while letting the guilty off scot-free. It is impossible for Him to be in the presence of sin in order to issue clemency for said transgression. An impartial ruling cannot be denied for the sake of pardon.

Only Jesus could reconcile such diametrically opposed characteristics of God. Only He could satisfy the righteousness so that mercy could be delivered to a guilty people. Only the Christ could bring together holiness and grace making both available to us.

This means that even though I am unrighteous and deserving of condemnation, I am free from such a guilty verdict and can walk in His forgiveness for the rest of my days. It also means that while I'm decidedly unholy in myself, even downright profane in comparison to the perfection of God, I am declared as clean and pure, a beneficiary of God's grace. Finally, it also means that even though I fall far short of God's glorious standard and rightfully earned His justice, l am freely absolved from any wrong doing. In His eyes, my sins no longer taint me and He is able to see me as He created me to be.

Through Christ Jesus I am able to fully experience God as my own Father, who is both to be respected and revered as a righteous, holy and just God as well as enjoyed in mercy, grace and loving forgiveness. While I may tend to keep my distance out of respect, He wants me to come close to love and adore Him. Only Jesus makes possible a joyful reverence for such a God as this!

> *It's hard to enjoy a God we fear*
> *but through Christ*
> *it's possible to fear Him with great joy.*

How do you keep your distance from God, thinking you could never be good enough to rest in His presence?

What difference does Jesus make in this line of thinking?

When do you fear God more than you love and adore Him?

Heavenly Father,

You are worthy to be praised and I want to give You my full respect and awe, but I often keep my distance out of reverence. Through Christ, You have made a way for me to enjoy Your presence in an intimate way. Help me to take advantage of such a benefit as this, drawing close and resting in You. I belong to You and I want to love You as You love me. Show me how my thinking about You is off so my relationship with You can become more intimate. I love You, Father, not because I should but because Your love is drawing me.

In Jesus' Name I pray, Amen

51

Faith that is to be Imitated

"Keep your lives free from the love of money and be content with what you have, because God has said, 'Never will I leave you; never will I forsake you.' So we say with confidence, 'The Lord is my helper; I will not be afraid. What can mere mortals do to me?' Remember your leaders, who spoke the word of God to you. Consider the outcome of their way of life and imitate their faith. Jesus Christ is the same yesterday and today and forever" (Hebrews 13:5-8).

There is believing, and then there is living that belief. Our faith can be kind of like playing dress-up, where we say all the things we think a follower of Christ would say, make the kind of decisions that seem pleasing to God and that line up with the Bible, avoid behaviors and practices that God warns us against in His Word, but does our faith go deeper than our mouth? Does it penetrate the marrow of our bones, piercing our hearts with conviction, transforming us supernaturally? Or is it just window dressing?

If our faith is real, more than just skin deep, the desires of our heart will change as time goes on. It's more than just breaking bad habits or practicing new disciplines. Rather, a devotion to the person of Jesus Christ will transform the way we think, give us a new value system, and turn our world upside down.

As we go through this transformation, what used to be important will lose its significance. The things we traditionally run after will shift to more kingdom-oriented pursuits. What previously got our motor running eventually becomes repulsive. This is the fruit of living in relationship with Jesus Christ as His disciple.

One of these indicators is how we feel about money and possessions. It is natural to be attracted to the trappings of this world, and most of us have at one time viewed money as a source of security, dreamed about winning the lottery and all we would buy with the sudden wealth, or wished for more than what we currently have, whether it be a nicer car, bigger house, or higher quality clothing. In some way, we've all been discontent with what we have.

This dissatisfaction is a sign that we are not taking God at His Word, that our faith is merely skin deep. It means, as a brother in Christ once said to me, that "it's time you put into action what you so boldly proclaim to be true." If we say we believe God is our Father and will provide for our needs and that He is faithful to stay with us no matter what, but then long for more than what He has given us, our faith is not transformative. It turns out to be only words we say but not truth upon which we rest.

Actions speak louder than words. For example, we know it is more powerful to see God's love in action than to simply hear the words that God loves us. Ask the homeless man whose hope was renewed by the hot meal and warm shelter in his hour of greatest need. Or the victim of spousal abuse who was at the end of her rope when an anonymous donor stepped in to support her until she could get on her feet. Or the child starving for love and affection who soaked in the attention of the young missionary. Each of these people experienced tangible evidence of God's love. Each learned the truth of the words, "God is love," by the faithfulness of these believers.

In the same way, living out our faith is a better testimony to the faithfulness of God and His ability to help us than a thousand sermons eloquently preached on the topic. To see the lack of fear as a woman faces life-ending cancer, or the deep happiness and serenity despite a man's poverty, or the willingness of a woman in the prime of her life to leave all worldly possessions behind in order to obey the call of God with complete and utter joy is to see faith that is lived out, belief that is more than skin deep, a trust in the promises of God that is genuine. This is the kind of living statement that changes lives. This is the kind of faith we can dare to imitate.

True faith is more than adhering to a religious regimen. True faith places all one's weight on the saving and transformative power of the Gospel of Jesus Christ, believing that Jesus is both our only hope and our best prospect.

How do you talk the talk but not walk the walk? In other words, would you characterize your faith as more of a relationship with a living God, or a dedication to a religion?

_____

_____

When does fear grip your heart, or discontent steal your peace, or doubt rule your decisions?

_____

_____

How can you tangibly prove your faith to be real, living out what you boldly proclaim as truth, instead of just letting them be only words that you say?

_____

_____

Heavenly Father,
    I know a lot about You and Your ways, but I admit that these truths often don't penetrate any deeper than my skin. Grow my faith, showing me how to live it out, trusting You with all aspects of my life. Give me a passion for Jesus, so that I want nothing more than to follow Him as my personal Shepherd. Give me a desire for kingdom

treasure as opposed to worldly wealth. Show me where I'm off, how I've failed to trust Your faithful promise to stay by my side and help me always. Thank you for Your patience as I learn to follow You wholeheartedly.
In Jesus' Name I pray, Amen

52
Colored by the Blood of Jesus

"Do not be carried away by all kinds of strange teachings. It is good for our hearts to be strengthened by grace, not by eating ceremonial foods, which is of no benefit to those who do so. We have an altar from which those who minister at the tabernacle have no right to eat. The high priest carries the blood of animals into the Most Holy Place as a sin offering, but the bodies are burned outside the camp. And so Jesus also suffered outside the city gate to make the people holy through his own blood. Let us, then, go to him outside the camp, bearing the disgrace he bore. For here we do not have an enduring city, but we are looking for the city that is to come.

Through Jesus, therefore, let us continually offer to God a sacrifice of praise—the fruit of lips that openly profess his name. And do not forget to do good and to share with others, for with such sacrifices God is pleased" (Hebrews 13:9-16).

Sacrifice was a filthy business. Flies buzzed around the blood and bits of flesh drying on the altar. The priests were covered in the smelly crimson fluid as it spattered everywhere, tainting their garments, skin, hair and sometimes even in their mouth if they weren't careful. Yesiree, sacrifice duty at the temple was not for the faint of heart.

Why would God require such a messy practice to deliver forgiveness to His people? And as if the blood were not enough, the very bodies of the animals that were being offered up to Him had to be laboriously carried outside the camp. Once there, the carcasses were burned completely so as not to taint the holy proceedings or the priests with the consumption of the meat as was the norm with other offerings, while the life-giving blood was used in the Holy of holies to atone for the sins of man. Forgiveness did not come easy.

There is the idea hidden in this passage that living for Christ is not clean, pretty, convenient or comfortable. He gave His life in the most horrific of ways, yes, but also in a demeaning and disgraceful way; on a Roman cross like a common criminal on the outskirts of town just as the animals of old were burned outside the camp. Perhaps it was God's intent to distinguish His sacrifice, so as not to be mistaken as just another martyr, or an addition to the belief system of the Jews, or as One who can be received as part of the package of the ways of this world. No, it's clear we must leave all that behind and go outside the city gates, so to speak, away from all expectations, all presumptions, all beliefs and look to His precious blood to atone for our sins. Equally as clear is the fact that sacrifice, even the one willingly given by Christ of His own flesh, was a messy affair, yet only the blood of Jesus can provide a way for our sins to be forgiven.

A.W. Tozer reminds us that, "Only the blood of Jesus can cleanse us, yet if we withhold ourselves from that blood, we will be unclean forever." And to be unclean is to be estranged from Holy God for all of eternity in a place of torment and suffering called Hell. Once cleansed, however, we are seen as righteous and holy for all eternity and are welcomed into His Presence with great love and acceptance. There we can look with all joyful anticipation to the city that is to come, the Jerusalem of new with gates of pearl and streets of gold. While here, however, in the nitty-gritty of daily living, we can walk in the cleanness His blood purchased for us and never neglect offering up our sacrifices of praise to the One who gave so much on our behalf. May we be colored by the blood of Jesus.

> *"Let us honor the blood of Jesus Christ every*
> *moment of our lives,*
> *And we will be sweet in our souls."*
> *—William J. Seymour*

In what ways do you try to stay above the fray of the world, neglecting to share the Good News of Jesus Christ to the lost all around?

_____

_____

When is it hard for you to get your hands dirty when coming alongside the lost in order to share Christ with them?

_____

_____

Heavenly Father,

I am so grateful for the shame and torture Your Son endured in order to spill His perfect blood to atone for my sins. I admit, I often think I am saved in order to live a blessed and comfortable life, forgetting that I'm called to follow Jesus into the mess. Help me to remember to keep the sacrifice of Jesus always on my mind so His blood colors all that I do and say.

In Jesus Name I pray, Amen

Cindy is a sinner plucked from the wide path and saved from certain destruction by the grace and mercy of her Lord and Savior Jesus Christ in dying on the cross where she placed her faith and found forgiveness and new life. She is passionate for God's Word and most enjoys seeing the impact God-breathed scripture has on those who study it. She is devoted to her husband of 30 years and is most grateful for him and the faith she sees in their four beautiful daughters.

29731521R10129

Made in the USA
San Bernardino, CA
18 March 2019